# DISTANCE EDUCATION AND THE MAINSTREAM

# DISTANCE EDUCATION AND THE MAINSTREAM

## CONVERGENCE IN EDUCATION

Edited by Peter Smith and Mavis Kelly

**CROOM HELM**
London • New York • Sydney

© 1987 Peter Smith and Mavis Kelly
Croom Helm Ltd, Provident House, Burrell Row,
Beckenham, Kent, BR3 1AT
Croom Helm Australia, 44-50 Waterloo Road,
North Ryde, 2113, New South Wales

Published in the USA by
Croom Helm
in association with Methuen, Inc.
29 West 35th Street,
New York, NY 10001

British Library Cataloguing in Publication Data

Distance education and the mainstream:
   convergence in education.
   1. Distance education
   I. Smith, Peter II. Kelly, Mavis
   371.3    LC5800
ISBN 0-7099-4499-3


Library of Congress Cataloging in Publication Data

ISBN 0-7099-4499-3

Printed and bound in Great Britain by Mackays of Chatham Ltd, Kent

# CONTENTS

## TABLES AND FIGURES

**Table**

**Figures**

# ACKNOWLEDGEMENTS

The idea for this book arose during the International Council for Distance Education Conference in Melbourne in August 1985. Peter Smith had just delivered a paper entitled *Distance Education: A Change Agent.* Over lunch Mavis Kelly remarked that she was very annoyed by the paper. 'Why?' 'Because I am half-way through writing it myself!' Two like minds do not justify a whole book on the subject of convergence between distance education and mainstream education but it did not take long to locate others who were thinking along the same lines. Happily the list of contributors to this volume reflects the international context in which it was conceived.

Not only were the editors separated by a considerable distance during the planning and preparation of the book, but contributors were scattered throughout the globe: in Africa, Australia, Britain, Canada and the United States of America.

Surprisingly, or perhaps not surprisingly, given that all contributors are experienced in distance education or other non-traditional forms of education, preparation of the book was accomplished without major crises of any kind and in a spirit of friendly co-operation.

We owe special thanks to the School of External Studies and Continuing Education, University of Queensland, Australia, which was prepared to underwrite the cost of preparing camera-ready copy for our publisher. Margaret Williams contributed to the process of editing manuscripts with characteristic thoroughness and flair, Edla Ward carried out all word processing and Ross Pulbrook assisted with illustration.

Camera-ready copy was produced on a VAX750 computer using the TROFF word-processing package and final copy was output on a Dec LN101 Laser Printer. Several contributors were able to supply diskettes which were transferred directly to computer memory. This eased the burden of keying text considerably.

Chapter Three, 'Bridging the Technology-Pedagogy Gap' by James W. Hall, was presented at the Thirteenth World Conference of the International Council for Distance Education, Melbourne, August 1985 under the title 'Telecommunications and the Technology/Pedagogy Gap' and was originally reproduced in the Conference Report. With some modifications, it is reproduced here with permission of the International Council for Distance Education.

Figure 3.1, The Pyramid of the Educated Person, appears in 'A Model College Education: From an Atraditional Viewpoint', by James W. Hall with Barbara L. Kevles, in *In Opposition to Core Curriculum: Alternative Models for Undergraduate Education*, James W. Hall, Ed., with Barbara L. Kevles, Greenwood Press, Westport, Ct., 1982, p. 205. Copyright (c) 1982 by James W. Hall and Barbara L. Kevles. Reprinted with permission of the copyright holders.

# INTRODUCTION

**Mavis Kelly and Peter Smith**

What will education be like in the year 2000 and beyond? The contributors to this book share a vision that it will differ from the present system in radical ways: in terms of access, methods used and the range of resources available for teaching and learning. In particular, the book focuses on trends which are blurring the boundaries between distance education and mainstream, campus-based education.

We realize that neither of these modes of education is homogeneous. Although we do not wish to mask the diversity that each mode embodies, we draw a distinction between them in terms of education which is primarily campus-based and education which is aimed primarily at students who do not attend a campus on a regular basis. The terms 'mainstream education' and 'campus-based education' are used interchangeably throughout the book. We use the term 'distance education' to refer to a range of titles which find expression world-wide: 'external studies'; 'extramural studies'; 'off-campus education'; 'correspondence education'.

We have deliberately avoided the use of adjectives like 'conventional' and 'traditional' to describe mainstream education, though clearly this mode of education does have a long and respected tradition. Likewise we do not use the terms 'non-traditional' or 'unconventional' to apply to distance education even though there is often a sense in which these descriptions are accurate.

We assume that distance education and mainstream education are located at the extremes of a continuum which is paralleled by the continuum showing the degree of face-to-face teacher support received by students: distance education students are assumed to receive less face-to-face support than campus-based students.

Orthogonal to this continuum is another which distinguishes open education from closed education. Open learning systems are assumed to be characterized by: open access; freedom from time constraints; choice of resources for learning; choice of learning strategies; and student control over assessment. Basically open systems are student-directed whereas closed systems are teacher-directed. We wish to maintain a neutral stance on the value of open and closed systems and regret that the term 'closed systems' has negative connotations. Hence we prefer to use the more neutral terms 'student-directed' and 'teacher-directed' to apply to the ends of this continuum.

We do not identify distance education with open learning in spite of the fact that terms like 'open university' and 'open campus programme' are in use world-wide. Institutions which adopt these titles usually lay claim to being open in terms of access and occasionally in terms of freedom from time constraints on students but in other ways they may be very closed.

Neither do we identify mainstream education with closed learning systems. Students who receive a high degree of teacher support may or may not be teacher-directed. The distinction that is now emerging in mainstream education between face-to-face teaching and resource-based teaching illustrates this point.

What do we mean by convergence? We discern three levels of convergence in current educational practice.

First, the methods of distance education and the methods of mainstream education are converging or becoming less distinguishable from each other. At the heart of this process is the evolution of teaching-learning systems which have fewer characteristics of campus-based education and more of the characteristics of distance education than has been the case previously. In addition systems designed for distance education students are incorporating some of the features of campus-based education.

At another level, the traditional clienteles served by each mode are changing and intermixing and are therefore beginning to converge.

At yet another level, distance education and mainstream education can be perceived to be both converging and moving towards becoming open learning systems.

The contributors to this book deal with several levels and types of education beyond the post-compulsory level. Hence all sectors of tertiary education are represented as well as various forms of continuing or lifelong education.

They also represent a variety of national viewpoints. This diversity reinforces our claim that convergence between distance education and mainstream education is a phenomenon worthy of attention.

We do not claim that convergence of distance education and mainstream education is a *fait accompli*. This would be far from the truth. What we present are some clear indications that convergence is beginning to occur both in theory and in practice. We believe that these trends are forerunners of a world-wide movement in education and training, which will set the pattern for future decades.

Central to convergence are the rapid advances in technology which facilitate one- and two-way communication as well as rapid data transmission.

The face-to-face delivery method, which characterizes mainstream education and training, evolved historically in rurally based societies where the literacy rate was low and people came together to hear from those who had books and could read. This method is less applicable in today's sophisticated Western societies, which have high rates of literacy and good resource distribution.

Distance education has its roots in the printing press, the mail system and the educational needs of geographically isolated, or highly mobile, populations. Twentieth century technological developments such as radio, television, telephone, audio- and video-cassettes, have influenced the original print delivery method.

Until recently face-to-face teaching has had the advantage of interactivity while distance education has had the disadvantage of lack of interactivity. However, modern communications technology is allowing the lack of interactivity in distance education to be overcome. Students are now able to interact with their institution and teachers on a real-time basis, and to access the institution's resources in a broader and more rapid sense. In the future the degree of access will increase and campus-based students will also be able to avail themselves of these channels of communication. There are already examples world-wide of campus-based courses set up entirely as independent learning programmes, with teaching staff acting as mentors and learning managers.

In spite of the optimism which accounts of convergence engender, it must be recognized that distance education is still clothed in some of the attitudes associated with its beginning as a makeshift and second-rate mode of education, to be resorted to when campus-based tuition was out of the question. In Chapter One, Jevons challenges these attitudes, arguing that while distance education has a different pattern of advantages and disadvantages from campus-based education, it has enough offsetting advantages to warrant a claim for parity of esteem. The single indisputable advantage is that distance education provides **access** to education regardless of geography, work or family commitments. It may also foster independence, allow for a more intimate interface with employment, permit a degree of control over the quality of instruction by virtue of its public nature, allow for improvement in instructional materials over time and foster staff awareness and development. In some instances there is also a significant cost advantage to education, primarily in terms of reduced capital expenditure.

Jevons cites the example of Deakin University in Victoria, Australia, where he was Vice-Chancellor in the first decade of its existence, as a case for institutional convergence. There, campus-based students are given the same study guides and have access to the same resources as distance education students. Classes conducted on the campus more closely resemble tutorials than face-to-face lectures.

4

The next two authors discuss distance education in terms of technological change, emphasizing its potential impact on mainstream education in Australia and the United States.

In Chapter Two, Peter Smith traces the recent growth of distance education in Australia. He places particular emphasis on its emergence as a sophisticated and forward looking form of education compared with its second-rate status in previous decades. He argues that its increasing popularity is, in part, attributable to changing social attitudes towards leisure and privacy and the enormous success of the British Open University, which has reflected on distance education world-wide. The potential exists now for distance education to impact on mainstream education because distance educators have been forced to develop and implement a wide range of teaching methods. In this sense it has moved forward at a faster pace than mainstream education and is well placed to act as a change agent, bringing with it examples of the effective use of new technologies.

When distance education meets highly institutionalized and highly structured mainstream education, however, they often arrive at an impasse and a stand-off occurs. The question which James Hall raises in Chapter Three, is how existing mainstream education can be modified to cope with distance education and the promise of technologically mediated learning systems that it brings with it. On the one hand, there is the desire to preserve the traditional strengths of universities and other institutions of higher education - scholarly research, teaching, and learning resources - while on the other, there is the need to extend these facilities to students regardless of their location. Mere access is not the issue here. As Hall points out, the challenge lies in using new technologies to stimulate learning at the highest levels. He calls this the **technology-pedagogy gap.**

Hall's solutions are imaginative and feasible in the 1980s. They include the use of electronic media to assist in course selection and to provide access to counsellors within institutions; access to the full range of courses of a university by all students; mentor support while studying via electronic mail; and flexibility in course entry and pacing.

5

Hall's concluding remarks are sobering though. In developed nations, the potential for an 'electronic university' exists but the demand is still relatively low because of the continued viability of mainstream education. In nations which are not so developed, the demand is exceedingly high but resources are modest and access to technology limited.

In Chapter Four, Barbara Matiru illustrates this point very well in her account of distance education in Kenya where a rise in the number of children entering primary education has placed severe strain on the pool of trained teachers. In addition to this the government's policy of raising the level of adult literacy has created a further need for trained teachers.

The media of instruction in distance education courses offered by the College of Adult and Distance Education in Kenya are print and radio broadcasts. It is a far cry from Hall's 'electronic university'. Distance education co-exists with traditional classrooms and lecture halls. There is evidence, however, that distance education materials are beginning to flow back into these campus-based settings and are in demand by classroom teachers and trainers.

The three chapters which follow on from Matiru's present examples of convergence in practice in Australia: in a technical and further education system (Foks), in industrial education and training (Ledwidge and Miller) and in a university (Ross).

In Chapter Five, Foks discusses the concept of open learning and the relationship between open learning and distance education. Open learning systems seek to provide students with as much choice and control as possible over course content and learning strategies. Distance education may or may not be open in that sense.

Open learning calls for small study units which can be combined or stand alone; educational objectives which are likely to meet students' needs; a variety of possible learning methods ranging from teacher-independent learning to immediate teacher-student interaction; and a choice of learning resources. The best learning methods may well be a mixture of face-to-face instruction and independent learning.

Foks goes on to provide a case study of the introduction of open learning in the Technical and Further Education sector in

Victoria, Australia. He also emphasizes the need for attitudinal, structural and procedural changes to implement open learning effectively. This is a formidable task requiring ingenuity and flexibility in both teaching and administration.

As Foks points out, in implementing open learning in dual-mode institutions there are dangers that distance education students as a group will not have enough attention focused on their particular needs. The solution which he recommends is to design programmes with distance education students as the primary target.

In Chapter Six, Ledwidge and Miller approach the issue of convergence from quite a different angle but one which is related to Foks' concerns. They begin their Chapter with a discussion of the divergent aims of the educational and industrial sectors. On the one hand, attainment of formal qualifications is the goal, on the other full mastery of skills is essential. Educational institutions can afford to fail a proportion of students or accept a level of attainment which is less than complete: industry cannot.

They discuss a number of issues which are pertinent to training the workforce effectively: collaboration between the industrial and educational sectors; appraising the needs of learners; ways of devising appropriate training programmes. In this context Ledwidge and Miller advocate distance education methods in preference to face-to-face instruction as a means of achieving flexible pacing, mastery of learning, wide access and fast improvement in competence levels in industry. Finally a number of schemes which would result in effective collaboration are cited. All of these require initiative but are quite feasible in the Australian context.

In Chapter Seven, Ross raises issues of both teaching method and course content relevant to the needs of part-time students. His discussion of the Humanities part-time programme at Griffith University in Queensland, Australia, has particular relevance to the issue of convergence since its founders set out to:

(1) Develop a completely new programme rather than one which was based on the existing full-time programme.

(2) Offer a sequence of small units, completion of which was marked by one successful assignment or examination.

(3) Replace face-to-face tuition entirely by packaged materials supplemented with tutorials.

(4) Set flexible dates for enrolment and submission of assignments to allow self-paced learning.

Naturally the degree of flexibility offered to students has presented problems in determining the style and content of tutorial discussions, in scheduling tutorials, and in providing accurate teaching-load figures.

The programme described by Ross has some open characteristics in course design and scheduling of progress as well as the obvious methodological similarities with distance education.

The final three chapters deal with specific issues arising from convergence of distance education and mainstream education. Paul and Sewart examine staff development needs, and Kelly sets out some barriers to convergence arising from administrative structures of mainstream education, principally funding and costing, academic teaching loads and systems of academic promotion; from staff and student perceptions of education; and from government agencies.

In Chapter Eight, Paul, at Athabasca University in Canada, examines the challenges to academic values posed by working in a university which teaches only at a distance. In particular, it challenges the three major elements in the role of academics: research; course preparation or development; and course presentation or delivery. The overriding challenge however is to the traditional autonomy of academics. Convergence means that academics in both campus-based and distance education universities must face these challenges. Paul cites instances of collaboration in Canada which mean that a higher proportion of academics are facing this issue.

In the first instance most academics in distance education universities were drawn from campus-based universities. Research, which is the hallmark of these universities, is a particularly difficult issue in distance education universities.

From Paul's analysis it appears that time management is the central issue here rather than lack of research time *per se*. Combined with the emphasis on institutional research as opposed to disciplinary research, academics are often faced with feelings of being disadvantaged with regard to their colleagues in campus-based universities.

Paul examines a range of academic staff development needs which might be addressed in order to alleviate some of the problems posed by working in distance education. The nature of the staff development programme which he recommends is, however, not a formal, structured one: rather it is based on the experience of developing and maintaining a course combined with peer group support.

In Chapter Nine, Sewart argues that generic differences between distance education and mainstream education have been emphasized unduly, while points of similarity and areas of overlap have generally been ignored. He assumes that teaching and learning are based on the same fundamental principles regardless of the mode of instruction.

The skills needed for two-way written communication, face-to-face tuition and counselling of students are fundamentally the same in both modes. Different institutional contexts may make specific demands on their teaching staff but the range of demands in mainstream education is so great as to overlap with the range of demands in distance education.

There is a growing awareness of staff development needs in higher education and this goes beyond the need for staff induction into teaching methods to the development of a harmonious relationship between teachers and institutions. Like Paul, Sewart recognizes that teachers in higher education will, in all probability, be required to teach in a variety of educational contexts during their lifetimes. The aim of an effective staff development programme is to equip them to do this.

While not wishing to conclude this book on a note of pessimism, in Chapter Ten, Kelly sets out some some barriers which need to be overcome in the implementation of plans for convergence.

Serious barriers exist within institutions in terms of organizational structures which have been established to administer mainstream education. Costing and funding systems do not take account of the fixed costs incurred in distance education or indeed in other forms of education in which course preparation is prolonged and does not vary as a function of student numbers. Alternative costing systems can, and have been developed based on activity costing. However, institutions in Australia which adopt these then face the problem that their systems are discrepant from those used to calculate government funding to institutions of higher education.

Allied to funding is the administrative structure within which academic teachers work. This determines their conditions of employment and level of employment in terms of promotion guidelines. It is true that departments and individuals do innovate in teaching methods but those who do so must often be prepared to accept that their efforts will not be recognized in any tangible way.

Students may themselves erect barriers to convergence. If distance education students view campus-based education as the norm and as a more desirable mode of education, or if they are unprepared to use technologies which are available for communication, then efforts to enhance their learning experience may meet with resistance.

Campus-based students too have set expectations about the experiences they will encounter in higher education. Campus-based education does not represent a radical departure from compulsory schooling in Australia and attempts to implement alternative teaching strategies such as resource-based teaching encounter difficulties with students' reactions unless they are carefully inducted into the programme.

Kelly argues that in Australia at least, government planners and funding agencies have continued to maintain a rigid distinction between distance education and campus-based education. Decisions which stem from this view may set the pattern of higher education in Australia in a way that makes convergence or indeed any kind of innovation within campus-based education extremely difficult.

In spite of the barriers that do exist we predict that convergence will continue and will gradually force changes on those groups who would prefer to maintain the *status quo*. In Western nations, a force which has yet to be reckoned with is the growing number of professionals who need to update their qualifications to keep pace with new technologies or to change career directions as new roles are created and others diminish in importance. Pragmatism rather than idealism may motivate new directions in higher education as was the case in early initiatives to set up provision for distance education students over a century ago.

The transition towards convergence of modes will doubtless be difficult but current trends indicate that it will occur.

## Chapter One

# DISTANCE EDUCATION AND CAMPUS-BASED EDUCATION: PARITY OF ESTEEM

**Fred Jevons**

Distance education should no longer be written off as second-best. It has a different pattern of advantages and disadvantages from campus-based education but it is not intrinsically inferior. Comparisons between these modes of education are too often set up in an unfair way by comparing distance education with a rosy myth of campus-based education as a system which never goes awry. Distance educators have been too much on the defensive, accepting the prevailing prejudices against this mode too readily.

Distance education has some advantages which should be recognized more widely: easier access; independent learning opportunities; a more intimate interface with employment; better quality control over course materials; the possibility of cumulative improvement in pedagogic quality; the staff development effect; and, under certain circumstances, lower costs.

While I am not arguing that distance education is as good as campus-based education in every possible way, I believe that distance education deserves parity of esteem. Recognition of the strengths and weaknesses of distance education as it is currently practised will open the door to using elements of both modes to the best effect for the benefit of students.

In short, I think it is time people stopped asking which mode is better. What an oversimplified question! They should ask what are the relative merits; under what circumstances and for what purposes is one mode to be preferred to the other; how could the advantages of each mode be combined; and so on.

12

The comparison should be approached with an assumption, not of equality, but of parity of esteem. Airing prejudices about the superiority of one mode over the other is not useful. It is better to look at the strengths and weaknesses of each, and work at improving standards in both.

It is all too easy to see why that is not the way most people approach the question. As usual, it is for the new to prove its worth. The old is taken for granted. And so the comparison is set up in a way which throws the onus of proof on distance education. There is a regrettable tendency to focus on a few obvious disadvantages of distance education and forget that campus-based education has many imperfections. Inevitably distance education will come off second-best if it is compared with a rosily nostalgic view of campus-based education in which there is never a timetable clash to restrict subject choice; in which no student and no teacher ever has an illness or a family crisis; in which every student participates eagerly in tutorials and avidly discusses work with other students late into the night; in which all teachers are in complete command over everything they teach and are adept in every pedagogic strategy and ruse. I once asked, 'if such a university exists, would someone please tell me where it is?' (Jevons, 1984a). So far I have had no response.

Higher education in Australia is funded mainly by the federal government. Attitudes of those in power have been traditionally relatively sympathetic to distance education, compared to those I have come across in some other countries, but only recently have they come close to acknowledging the ideal of parity of esteem for which I am arguing here. In its most recent pronouncement on the subject, the Australian Commonwealth Tertiary Education Commission expresses what is nearly a parity standpoint. In the *Review of Efficiency and Effectiveness in Higher Education* (1986) it concludes that 'external studies courses have an important role to play ... in promoting access and equity ... . It is not however an appropriate mode for all types of training ... and it may not be suitable for all students ... . Contact with other students and staff is an important aspect of learning and the external mode limits such contact' (p. 238). All that is missing here is to add

13

that neither is campus-based education suitable for all students.

Contact with other students and staff! That is the great shibboleth with which distance educators have to contend. Sometimes the objection is based on sheer misunderstanding - the mistaken notion that distance education students are somehow forbidden or prevented from having contact with other students and staff, whether face-to-face, by telephone or through some other medium. This misunderstanding can be cleared up by mere explanation of the opportunities for contact which are built into good distance education systems.

The real difficulty of the issue goes deeper: should students be **required** to have such contacts? This is a controversial question. One has to respect the good intentions of those who want not only to lead the horse to the water but also to make it drink. They know how greatly many students appreciate personal contact. But it is a big step - as a matter of social philosophy, not only of educational technique - that separates opportunities for many from compulsion for all.

There is a great variety of students to consider. They range from octogenarians to prisoners to mobile young executives to shift workers, not to mention the legendary lighthouse keepers. To the variety of students, and the variety of circumstances in which they study, has to be added the great diversity of preferred learning methods. There are many ways to help students to learn (and teaching can never be more than that). Some of these ways depend on face-to-face contact, but others do not. I am not persuaded that it is good or justifiable to impose one particular method as a prerequisite for all who want to learn. If there are some individuals who want to learn on their own, their preferences should be respected as far as possible.

The rapid advances in technology have opened up new options for interaction between staff and students, and have lifted constraints that previously seemed unavoidable. The campus-based mode with its emphasis on the face-to-face method of tuition may still be the norm, but if today's technology is used well alternatives to it may be as good or better, depending on the circumstances.

## Advantages of Distance Education

From the way in which I have set out the problem, it follows that it is not incumbent on me to set out the advantages of campus-based education. The superiority of campus-based education is the conventional wisdom, so I don't need to put that side of the case. I want to challenge that conventional wisdom, and for that purpose I have to make good my claim that distance education has enough offsetting advantages to warrant the claim for parity of esteem.

The following list of seven advantages of distance education is an expanded version of what I have argued on previous occasions (Jevons 1984a,b).

### Access

Even those who regard distance education as a makeshift second-best alternative accept that, because of the flexibility it offers and the relief it gives from constraints of timing and location, it widens access to education. Distance education is a feasible option for many people for whom campus-based education is difficult or impossible. There is a whole range of barriers to campus-based education which are absent or lower in the case of distance education. They include geographical isolation, family commitments and the requirements of employment.

It is sometimes argued that students opt for distance education only because it is more 'convenient' and that the choice reflects lower commitment. The assumption seems to be that time spent travelling to evening classes is a measure of commitment. It is an imperfect measure at best, and in any case, distance from the nearest campus offering the programme is only one of many possible barriers. Clearly physical barriers to access should be lowered as far as it is practicable to do so, because they affect individuals very differently for reasons which have nothing to do with education. If measures of commitment are sought for use as selection criteria, it is not safe to rely on such ambiguous ones.

**Self-directed Learning**

Because of their separation from the teacher, distance education students approach more closely the ideal of the autonomous learner. Of course they do not always do so in practice, but it can be argued that the circumstances are more conducive for them to do so.

**A more Intimate Interface with Employment**

Students who have jobs do not have to leave them to study by distance education. There is less disjunction, therefore, between the context of work and the context of study, and it is easier for students to relate one to the other. Distance education shares this advantage with part-time, campus-based education, but for this mode the geographical constraint is tight. You cannot be a part-time, campus-based student unless you are within easy reach of a campus.

**Quality Control**

Everybody knows that, even in the best institutions, not everything in campus-based education is excellent. There is an extraordinary tendency to forget this as soon as the comparison with distance education is raised. What goes on in the privacy of tutorials is one of the great mysteries of the natural history of campuses. Some of it is doubtless excellent, but what is not excellent may not be heard about until it approaches scandal proportions, and even then it tends to be talked about in whispers. Student evaluation of teaching helps, but is not infallible. Even in the relatively public forum of the lecture, quality control is not all it might be. The lecturer's words vanish into thin air within an instant, and are not normally available for later scrutiny and criticism.

It is different in distance education. Every academic who turns to preparing materials for distance education students knows what a difference it makes that the materials will be in the public domain. That, perhaps, is why the course team method of operation 'took' so readily when it was introduced at

Deakin University in Australia in the late seventies. To have one's drafts criticized by colleagues can be traumatic, but to be criticized publicly later may be worse.

## Cumulative Improvement

The opportunity for cumulative improvement in pedagogic quality follows from quality control. Distance education materials have a permanent physical existence; that is, they are objective knowledge in the sense that Karl Popper (1979) used that expression. They are subject to criticism, and open to improvement through criticism. In my view, a major challenge for distance education is to make the most of the opportunity of getting feedback from students who use the materials and from other sources.

Campus-based lectures do not offer the same opportunity. Lectures may be conscientiously revised year by year, but the quality of lectures is not, in my experience, better on average now than it was thirty years ago. I see updating, but I do not see sustained improvement comparable with the improvement in the general level of quality of distance education materials in the last two decades.

## The Staff Development Effect

Another consequence of quality control is that the discipline of preparing distance education materials is stricter than that of preparing and presenting lectures. When you know you are going to appear in print, it concentrates the mind wonderfully.

Especially salutary is the effect of working in course teams. Few who have worked in a course team can have escaped unscathed by new ideas and approaches. From other subject experts in the team one may develop new approaches to the subject matter. From those same colleagues, or from instructional designers working with the team, one may develop ideas on how to expand the repertoire of techniques for preparation, presentation, and assessment.

## Cost

This is a tricky point. Where student numbers are large, there are economies of scale because the high initial cost of preparing distance education materials can be spread across a large number of students. The cost structure of distance education, as compared with campus-based education, is characterized by higher fixed and lower variable costs.

Authorities in developing nations have opted for distance education because it seemed the only affordable way to expand the provision of education for the large numbers still excluded from it.

But 'selling' distance education on the basis that it is cheap is a two-edged sword. If the system, once established, has to be run on the cheap, the quality of the materials, and the extent of student support, are bound to suffer. In Australian conditions, the Commonwealth Tertiary Education Commission (1986, p.227) has suggested that efficiency in terms of unit costs is reached when enrolments in a subject are above a threshold which lies between 50 and 150.

Those, then, are seven advantages of distance education which challenge the conventional wisdom that campus-based education is superior. They are not all unambiguous and they impinge differently on the different groups involved in the processes of education. But cumulatively I think they destroy the case for assuming, without further ado, that campus-based education is best and is the preferred mode wherever it is not quite impossible. Distance education should be seen as a fully viable alternative to campus-based education, and there should be no *a priori* assumption in favour of campus-based education, either by providers or by consumers of education.

That is the ideal. Of course I recognize that it is not likely to be fully realized in practice for a long time, but I do think it is a reasonable ideal to aim at.

# Is the Parity Argument being Superseded?

Looking to the future, I wonder - is the argument about parity going to be superseded by events? To some extent I think it may be because of growing moves towards convergence between distance education and campus-based education. In the medium to long term, I believe the two modes will become more like each other both in the methods they use and in the clienteles they serve.

## Convergence of Methods

There used to be stories of a 'black market' in 'external notes'. Institutions which taught in both modes wanted the campus-based students to attend classes, and so they tried to stop them getting hold of the notes prepared for the distance education students. Hence the black market - because, of course, the campus-based students found the notes useful. When, for any of a number of good or bad reasons, they missed a lecture or two, they could catch up from the 'external notes'. Even if they did not miss lectures, the notes prepared for the distance education students were more reliable than the notes they could take themselves in lectures. Remember the old joke about lectures? 'Lectures are a way to transfer material from the lecturer's notes to the students' notes without passing through the mind of either'.

Deakin University in Australia was, as far as I am aware, the first to turn the black market into an official policy. Having lavished so much staff time on the course teams which drafted the study guides, having poured precious resources into editing, design and printing, it seemed silly to have the staff stand in front of their classes and hold forth as though those lovingly prepared course materials did not exist. So campus-based students were given the course materials, and classes held on the campus became more like tutorials in support of them. It was named the 'Open Campus Program'.

Already, there has been a marked blurring of the boundary between distance education and campus-based education. There is little that can be done away from a campus that

19

cannot also be done on a campus, and campus-based education is likely to make increasing use of the advances achieved in distance education. Walking around campuses these days one sees more and more students sitting in front of computer terminals. Why do they need to come to the campus to do that? Anything digital can go up and down a telephone line with the greatest of ease.

The 'open learning' movement is a sign that the convergence of activities on- and off-campus is already under way. The further it proceeds, the more the question of parity will become emptied of significance.

## Convergence of Clienteles

The dogma used to be that campus-based universities were for school leavers and that adults who wanted a degree were a different clientele needing a different kind of provision. It was for them that distance education universities were created. I went to Birmingham in 1979 for the Conference on the Education of Adults at a Distance with a paper which argued that distance education students are not so very different from campus-based students. I thought a little touch of unorthodoxy might generate discussion. I was disappointed! My argument was not disputed - it was just ignored. People did not want to know. The conference was dominated by the charismatic British Open University and its various single-mode clones around the world. They claimed to be doing a different job for a different category of students. Their very *raison d'être* depended on the difference. It was not a matter for disputation, it was an article of faith.

The basis for the belief was the situation in the United Kingdom. Universities there had run down their part-time provision to such an extent that, for most adults, the Open University was their only avenue to a degree.

For school leavers, the Open University's Younger Student Pilot Scheme, launched in its early years, was evaluated and found to have been, at best, a very equivocal success (Woodley and McIntosh, 1980). It was concluded that distance education is not suitable for school leavers, or at least that school leavers require a different and more generous support system to achieve success rates comparable to those of adult Open University students.

So immense was the influence of the Open University that pragmatic, country-specific decisions almost became a world-wide dogma.

It was such a neat scheme of differentiation! Distance education for adults, campus-based education for school leavers. But the factual basis for it was thin, and there was something strange about the argument. The distance education mode is used to provide a major part of secondary education in many developing countries. In Australia there are well-established correspondence schools offering secondary and even primary level education. Why should distance education not be suitable for an intermediate age range when it can demonstrably be made to work for both younger and older students?

The school leaver question needs to be re-examined, as John Anwyl and his colleagues at the University of Melbourne have argued persuasively (Anwyl, Powles and Patrick, 1986). In Australia, opinions held by academics about school leavers enrolling for higher education by distance education range from outright rejection to unconditional acceptance. Those who oppose such enrolments tend to cite the British Open University's experience. Those who favour them point to the fact that there are already substantial numbers of younger students studying by distance education in Australian universities and colleges of advanced education. As Anwyl and his colleagues point out, the matter may become a major policy issue before long, because there are suggestions that distance education may be called on to help meet the expanding demand for higher education which may result from increased retention of students in schools to Year 12. Then it will be important to know more about it. Are there some types of students for whom it is more suitable? Are there techniques that are particularly applicable - those, for instance, which use modern technologies to which children often take much more readily than adults? What kind of support systems are called for? Is there a case for mixing distance education with campus-based

21

education, in either a concurrent or an alternating way?

The important point for my argument here is that it is no longer generally accepted that distance education is not for school leavers. Differentiation by age group shows signs of breaking down, and this boundary line, which once seemed to separate distance education quite sharply from campus-based education, is becoming hazy.

In conclusion, let me add a few remarks about the nature of my arguments. They are normative and futuristic.

The parity of esteem thesis is clearly normative, not descriptive. It is not the case - yet - that most people think distance education is as good as campus-based education. From the nature of the parity argument it follows that there can be no objection to people preferring campus-based education - as long as their preference is a well informed and reasoned one. But to the extent that it is based on prejudice, or on ignorance of what distance education now is and can now do, it is a pity, because it means that those people are not making the most of their chances. It is all the more a pity when the prejudice or ignorance is shown by educational authorities or administrators, because those people are making other people's choices for them.

The convergence argument is one about the future, medium to long term. There are signs that convergence is beginning to happen, but it is going to take a long time.

If things turn out as I have suggested they might, will distance education have won a great victory by, in effect, taking over much of campus-based education? Or will distance education be like an inventor and entrepreneur who, having worked hard to establish an innovation, finds it taken up by a giant multinational and has to watch others making their fame and fortune from it? If the latter, distance education will have to content itself with a non-material reward - the satisfaction of knowing that it led the way.

# References

Anwyl, J., Powles, M. and Patrick, K. (1986) *Who Uses*

*External Studies? Who Should?*, report to the Standing Committee on External Studies, Commonwealth Tertiary Education Commission, Canberra

Commonwealth Tertiary Education Commission (1986) *Review of Efficiency and Effectiveness in Higher Education*, Australian Government Publishing Service, Canberra

Jevons, F.R. (1984a) 'Distance Education in a Mixed Institution: Working Towards Parity', *Distance Education*, 5, 1, 24-37

Jevons, F.R. (1984b) 'The Role of Distance Education: Towards Parity of Esteem' in T. Craig (ed.), *Technology Innovation: University Roles*, Association of Commonwealth Universities, London, pp. 343-9

Popper, K.R. (1979) *Objective Knowledge: An Evolutionary Approach*, Clarendon Press, Oxford

Woodley, A. and McIntosh, N.E. (1980) *The Door Stood Open: An Evaluation of the Open University Younger Student Pilot Scheme*, Open University, Milton Keynes

**Fred R. Jevons**, MA PhD *Cant.*, DSc HonDSc *Manc.*,
Hon D Univ *Open*, HonDLitt *Deakin*

Emeritus Professor
Deakin University
Australia

## Chapter Two

# DISTANCE EDUCATION AND EDUCATIONAL CHANGE

**Peter Smith**

Over the past fifteen years in Australia, there has been increased interest and participation in distance education. This is attributable to social change as well as to increased acceptance of the quality of this mode of education.

The increased esteem for distance education is related, at least partly, to greater sophistication and flexibility of teaching methods which have been facilitated by the effective use of new technologies. Generally, distance educators have been more willing to adopt new teaching methods than have campus-based educators. In this sense distance education has moved forward at a faster pace than mainstream education. However, the method changes and advances in distance education are now being utilized by some campus-based teachers, with the result that mainstream and distance education are drawing closer together. I predict that the two modes will converge to a point where they become far less distinguishable than they are at present in terms of materials design, organizational response, curriculum delivery, and student learning activities. It is my belief that distance education will be the major change agent in this convergence process, partly through the necessity for better delivery methods and the consequent opportunity for interactivity between institutions and remote students, and partly because it is not yet so institutionalized that it has ceased to be laterally thinking, or needs to protect an entrenched establishment.

## Distance Education in the Post-Compulsory Education Sectors

In Australia there are three sectors of post-compulsory education:

(1) The University sector ranges from the baccalaureate to the doctoral level.

(2) The College of Advanced Education sector ranges from two-year, full-time associate diplomas to the baccalaureate level, although some colleges do offer masters programmes. These programmes are designed to be more 'vocational' than 'theoretical'.

(3) The Technical and Further Education (TAFE) sector offers programmes for apprenticeship to certificate level, where the latter is similar to an associate diploma in a college.

Distance education at the compulsory schooling and TAFE levels has been available in all Australian states for many years. Prior to 1970 however, significant distance education programmes were only offered through four institutions of higher education. By 1986 there were twelve colleges offering distance education, each with a wide range of programmes. Regional colleges, located in rural towns and cities, comprise seven of the twelve major providers. These colleges developed distance education programmes vigorously because there was insufficient local population to yield large numbers of campus-based students. There are now five universities offering wide ranges of programmes by distance education. In addition to these major providers, there are a number of colleges offering a limited range of specialist courses by distance education.

**Table 2.1:** Australian Higher Education Enrolments, 1975-1985

| Year | Full-time internal enrolments | | Part-time internal enrolments | | External enrolments | |
|------|------|------|------|------|------|------|
| | No. | % total | No. | % total | No. | % total |
| UNIVERSITIES | | | | | | |
| 1975 | 96,669 | 65.4 | 42,194 | 28.6 | 8,891 | 6.0 |
| 1977 | 102,431 | 64.9 | 45,808 | 29.0 | 9,680 | 6.1 |
| 1979 | 98,249 | 61.4 | 48,890 | 30.5 | 13,003 | 8.1 |
| 1981 | 99,027 | 59.6 | 51,434 | 31.0 | 15,571 | 9.4 |
| 1982 | 99,324 | 59.6 | 51,868 | 31.1 | 15,497 | 9.3 |
| 1983 | 102,117 | 60.5 | 51,209 | 30.4 | 15,313 | 9.1 |
| 1984 | 105,369 | 61.2 | 50,649 | 29.5 | 15,972 | 9.3 |
| 1985 | 106,805 | 61.1 | 51,528 | 29.5 | 16,484 | 9.4 |
| COLLEGES OF ADVANCED EDUCATION | | | | | | |
| 1975 | 77,037 | 61.4 | 39,980 | 31.9 | 8,366 | 6.7 |
| 1977 | 85,468 | 59.8 | 46,556 | 32.6 | 10,892 | 7.6 |
| 1979 | 83,600 | 52.2 | 59,141 | 36.9 | 17,368 | 10.8 |
| 1981 | 76,685 | 46.5 | 64,913 | 39.3 | 23,469 | 14.2 |
| 1982 | 77,795 | 46.2 | 65,992 | 39.1 | 24,801 | 14.7 |
| 1983 | 82,717 | 47.7 | 65,374 | 37.8 | 25,192 | 14.5 |
| 1984 | 86,234 | 48.5 | 65,115 | 36.6 | 26,530 | 14.9 |
| 1985 | 93,213 | 49.8 | 65,802 | 35.1 | 28,280 | 15.1 |

Source: Compiled from Commonwealth Tertiary Education Commission Statistical Reports, 1975-1985

## Reasons for the Growth of Distance Education

Table 2.1 indicates the growth in numbers of distance education students in universities and colleges since 1975. It clearly shows that the number of such students has doubled in the universities, and trebled in the colleges, over the ten year period from 1975 to 1985. While it is not possible to give accurate statistics for the TAFE sector, the numbers of distance education students has also increased dramatically in the same ten year period, and there are currently more than 55,000 students enrolled in TAFE distance education programmes.

In a report prepared for the Commonwealth Tertiary Education Commission, Johnson (1983) concluded that the major reasons for the growth of distance education in Australia lay in:

(1) The need to upgrade qualifications in response to technological change.

(2) The convenience of distance study as opposed to part-time, campus-based study.

(3) The changing status of women in our society.

Two other reasons may be added to Johnson's list: respectability of study in the distance education mode and trends towards privacy in our society.

Each of the reasons for the growth in distance education will now be considered in more detail.

### Upgrading Qualifications in Response to Technological Change

Quite clearly the vocational employment pattern in Western society will change substantially by the year 2000. For example, data collected by Australia's Commission for the Future indicates substantial growth in the percentage of the workforce employed in the service industries of: recreation;

personnel and entertainment services; education; health and community services; finance; property and business services. The same data indicate a decline in the percentage of the workforce in: wholesale and retail trade; manufacturing; agriculture; forestry; fishing and hunting. Education and training requirements in the expanding areas will be enormous compared with the declining areas.

Without massive increases in capital and recurrent expenditure, it is doubtful that mainstream education will be able to respond rapidly enough to these needs. Also, more and more people who are already in employment are finding that advances in technology are such that they cannot acquire appropriate skills simply through on-the-job experience. These people need to be able to upgrade their skills without going back to full-time study. Although part-time, campus-based study is one alternative, many find the distance education mode more convenient.

## Convenience of Distance Education as Opposed to Part-time, Campus-based Study

During the 1950s a typical part-time student attended an inner city institution after work for some hours of lectures or tutorials and for library study. That was before television, before widespread affluence, and before people became concerned about being in the city at night. The alternative of 'correspondence' study was a poor one indeed. Availability was not good. Notes were often handouts which had been given to campus-based students, stapled together, with advice to read the textbook, and come to the examination.

During the 1970s people were able to participate in a greater variety of leisure-time activity. It became more distasteful to battle increasing cross-town traffic and find a parking space to attend evening lectures. The alternative of distance education became more attractive, since it allowed for flexibility that fitted well with modern lifestyles. Distance education meant that a student could go home after work, play with the children, watch TV, maintain a social and community life, and timetable study to fit with these other demands.

In the mid-1980s all Australian distance education providers in the higher education sector report that between forty and sixty per cent of their students reside in capital cities. These cities are well-endowed with institutions of higher education where students could attend a campus on a part-time basis if they wished.

## The Changing Status of Women

As Johnson (1983) suggested, the changing status and aspirations of women have added to the growth of tertiary education in general and, therefore, to distance education.

In 1981 women comprised 49.3 per cent of distance education students at university level, while only 42.2 per cent of the campus-based students were women. In the colleges of advanced education, 47.2 per cent of distance students were women, and 48.4 per cent of internal students were women.

## The Respectability of Distance Education

At the time that the University of New England commenced its distance education programme in 1955, it was considered to be a second-rate mode of higher education. It was substantially for that reason that the University of New England adopted the so-called 'integrated' model of education, (where the staff teach the same courses, both internally and externally), to ensure that the academic experience and demands placed upon distance education students were as similar as possible to those of their campus-based counterparts.

The assumption that distance education is inferior has been largely dispelled, partly through the quality of distance education graduates, and partly by the imaginative use of new technologies. The technologies principally used in distance education in recent times include sophisticated instructional design; cheap and flexible offset printing; well designed and produced audio-cassettes; and telephone tutorials.

In the past few years some institutions have been using video-cassettes, satellite transmissions, and microcomputers. More use is beginning to be made, as the land-based telephone system improves, of remote terminals connected to mainframe computers, running computer assisted instruction (CAI) and computer managed learning (CML) software.

The advent of the British Open University added academic respectability to distance education, lending moral support and confidence to teaching staff and administrators involved in distance education, to the students using the mode, and to the wider community that needs to have confidence in this mode of education. It is important to note here that the Open University won its reputation for excellence largely on the basis of its use of educational technology in its broadest sense.

**Trends Towards Privacy in Our Society**

Distance education is congruent with the increasingly private nature of lifestyles in Western society, as discussed by Pawley (1973) and Toffler (1981). The argument that lifestyles are becoming increasingly private is based on the observation that affluence and technology allow us to access many things in our homes that once were only accessible by leaving them.

It is interesting to look at a few examples of this trend towards more private living. Plumbing and drainage have had a major effect. Where the village well was a publicly-shared utility (and still is in the developing world), we now have taps in our own homes. Where once toilets were shared, we now have these in our homes. People no longer need to leave home for these utilities and therefore no longer experience human contact in the process.

More recently, radio has enabled us to access news and entertainment without leaving home. Television has, of course, added new dimensions to what radio started. Telephones have enabled us to carry out a good deal of our business and interpersonal interaction without leaving home. The motor car has enabled us to move around in privacy. Most recently, computers and videotex have enabled us to access and interact privately with even more information.

Whether it be home swimming pools or video-cassette recorders, wherever a product has enabled a previously public act to be carried out in the convenience and privacy of home (or work), that product has been a success. Distance education is such a product.

In examining the reasons for the growth of distance education in the last ten years, mention must also be made of the fact that, by 1975, the products of the post-war baby boom were well into their twenties and reaching their thirties by the 1980s. Many in this group who missed out on a post-compulsory education in their late teens now aspire to a higher education. While this alone does not explain the explosive growth of distance education relative to part-time, campus-based enrolments, it is a factor to be taken into consideration.

# Impact of Distance Education on Methods of Teaching and Learning

It is possible to argue that the growth of distance education has had a significant effect on the methods of teaching and learning in all sectors of higher education in Australia. The claim is often made by proponents of the 'integrated' model of education that campus-based teaching is improved by the more rigorous requirements of distance teaching (Smith 1979, Laverty 1980, Cross 1980).

As would be expected, this claim is not often disputed in distance education circles, nor in the literature. Certainly, ample practical evidence can be adduced to support it. There are, however, other views on this issue, some of which will be addressed later in this Chapter.

First, though, let us address some of the reasons that distance educators put forward to support the claim, not only that distance education has had a significant effect on campus-based teaching and learning, but that this effect has been a positive one.

## Use of Alternative Teaching Methods

Distance educators have been forced, through necessity, to consider alternative teaching methods simply because traditional face-to-face methods are not available to them.

31

They have had to optimize the use of print, graphics and, more recently, of audio-cassettes. The need to look at alternatives has led to a critical stance being adopted on all methodologies. Distance teachers have been more ready than campus-based teachers to experiment with personalized systems and instruction, video-cassettes, telephone tuition, home computers and satellites. They have been more ready to experiment largely because they have had to be.

Rumble and Keegan (1982) tabulated thirteen kinds of media used in distance education: print, study centres, face-to-face tuition, telephone tuition, computer assisted instruction, access to computer terminals, access to laboratories at study centres, home experiment kits, residential schools, television, videotapes, radio and audio-cassettes. There are two particularly interesting features about this list:

(1) It is a more extensive list than one will find in use in campus-based teaching.

(2) There is evidence that institutions engaged in distance education as well as campus-based education have made more use of this range of techniques among their campus-based students.

Typical delivery methods in mainstream and other modes of education in the TAFE sector were tabulated by McBeath (1985). Her analysis reveals that mainstream modes of instruction are much more limited in the range of resources and media available to students than other modes, including distance education. This is consistent with Rumble and Keegan's (1982) findings.

Distance education has also had a major part to play in the development of course materials used in higher education: distance education offers the opportunity of cumulative improvement in the quality of teaching.

On the other hand, some would want to argue that distance education has detracted from the quality of post-compulsory education.

The first sort of argument is that the face-to-face method of instruction is the most effective method available. Nobody who has experienced good and stimulating face-to-face instruction would wish to deny the power of that instruction. Nor would it be easy to substitute for it.

Distance educators frequently resort to face-to-face instruction in regional tutorials, and campus-based residential schools. In some disciplines these experiences are clearly more important than others in promoting insight and understanding of the subject.

Some authors (e.g. Holmberg 1976) have claimed that the face-to-face method is important in achieving some aspects of academic socialization. Research in this area is proceeding, but what is important here is recognition that not all academic objectives can be met equally well by distance education as it is currently practised. It is likely too that campus-based education will meet some other objectives less well than distance education.

## Overcoming the 'Closed' Nature of Distance Education

The second sort of argument is that made by Romiszowski (1981) who identifies a spectrum which has the 'free discovery' movement at one end. That movement, Romiszowski argues, is characterized by the view that learners should establish their own aims, with minimal guidance from the teacher, and should merely be given the resources required to discover the means of achieving them. At the other end of the spectrum are '... the various multi-media, personalised or resource-based schemes which ... offer the learner a variety of pre-prepared paths towards predetermined goals' (p. 3). Such extremes have been characterized as open and closed learning systems.

It is the latter end of the spectrum that most closely characterizes modern distance education, which is criticized by 'free discovery' educators and by educators whose views lie elsewhere along the spectrum postulated by Romiszowski. Such criticism acknowledges that distance education places constraints upon the openness of learning systems. For example, in the context of teaching mathematics, MacDonald

33

(1976) drew attention to the potential difficulties of distance education methods for campus-based students. MacDonald argued that when students cannot see mathematical proofs being formed in front of their own eyes their learning experience is degraded. Additionally, MacDonald argued, distance education students are denied the experience of starting off on a chain of deductive reasoning only to be told to go back to a certain point and argue from a different perspective. In MacDonald's words, 'This second (and vital) aspect of learning is almost unconsciously mediated every time a lecturer or tutor waves his hands and says ... "Wait a minute. If you do this, then such and such, so let's do so and so"' (p. 76).

However, new interactive technologies will enable some (if not all) of the concerns expressed by MacDonald to be addressed by distance educators. This should enable distance education to move towards being an open learning as opposed to a closed learning system. The tendency to herd learners down a fairly narrow pathway and to pre-programme learning experiences should be diminished when education is coupled with new technologies. As distance education becomes more open, opportunities for the application of distance education methods in campus-based education will increase.

## Use of Technology by Distance Educators

Those distance educators fortunate enough to go to the International Council of Distance Education World Conference in Vancouver in 1982 were able to see first hand, in a sharply defined and dazzling way, the sophisticated use and further potential of technologies such as broad-band satellite and cable television in distance education. There was a clear spin-off from these technologies to the broader spectrum of education in Canada. The Knowledge Network of the West (KNOW) and TV Ontario enthused us in particular.

In the first instance, it was the needs of isolated students in the compulsory years of schooling that brought television and video to education in Australia. In the 1960's television was used as a means of bringing centralized visual resources to primary and secondary schools in the cities, the heavily populated rural areas, and those areas of the remote outback that had access to broadcast television.

Subsequently, distance educators pioneered the use of the NASA Satellite ATS-1 for educational purposes at the post-compulsory level. At the University of the South Pacific, in the early 1970s, the requirements of distance education encouraged that University to make use of the PEACESAT satellite network to reach students who were scattered throughout a region where other forms of communication were inadequate to meet their needs.

In August 1983, the Kangaroo Network Bulletin listed PEACESAT Ground Stations, and there were seven in operation in Australia at that time. Of these, five belonged to institutions concerned with distance education. In August 1983 a further eighteen stations were awaiting commission. Of these, eleven were being built by institutions with a major commitment to distance education. Of the remaining seven, four were commissioned by state or federal police, one by the Bureau of Meteorology, and two by other educational institutions that have a minor commitment to distance education.

In other words, distance educators were early to pick up on ATS-1 after its westward shift of footprint, and they are clearly showing the way in Australian education. Additionally, it was distance educators who, soon after the footprint shift, commenced the Tertiary Distance Education Network on Kangaroo, to use ATS-1 to gain experience in satellite technology and to plan for AUSSAT which was to be launched in August 1985.

Early in 1985, ATS-1 shifted eastward and Australia went out of the footprint. We lost a very cheap source of communication and satellite experience. In educational circles it was distance educators who showed greatest interest in AUSSAT. While it may seem obvious, it did not have to be so. There are many other possible applications of the satellite for campus-based teaching such as communication between academics and administrators; accessing teaching expertise among institutions; computer communications; inter-library

35

loans; library networks and so on. It seemed so natural for distance education institutions to be interested and for the others not to be. The fact that it seemed natural is hard to interpret, but it may be simply that distance educators saw a more obvious application, and are predisposed to a search for better ways to ply their trade.

The penetration of new technology into most households in the form of radio, television, audio- and video-cassette players also gave impetus to distance educators to make use of this technology for educational purposes.

By the early 1970s cassette players were owned widely enough in the community that distance educators could start, with some care, to use them quite often. By the middle seventies they were used as a matter of course - most households had a cassette player and, in any event, they were cheap enough that students could be expected to buy one. By 1986, video-cassettes are at least widespread in the resource centres of most institutions, and a selection of computer software is appearing as well. Australian Bureau of Statistics figures indicate that, at the end of 1985, 38 per cent of Australian households owned video-cassette players.

In 1977, there was one home computer shop in the United States. Most Australian towns now have at least one. Distance educators were quick to start using personal computers as part of self-instructional packages for use in the home. However, these can only be used in accredited courses as supplementary materials, since access is still not widespread enough. It is worthwhile noting, however, that the 1986 Australian price of around $1650 for an IBM PC compatible, with 640k RAM, twin disk drives, and colour monitor, is less in real terms than a black and white television set was in 1960.

It cannot be argued that distance educators pioneered the use of personal computers in post-compulsory education. What can be argued, though, is that the nature of the material produced for computer-based education, and the individualized and interactive nature of its use by students, is identical for both campus-based and distance education students.

The same argument can be made about the use in education of other modern technologies, such as offset print, and video-disc. It is not that distance educators pioneered the use of these technologies. It is the nature of the material produced through these technologies, and the use of these materials by teachers and students that is important, since these are the same both for campus-based and for distance education students.

## Technology and Convergence in Education

Effective use of new technologies can lead to a situation where remote students can communicate with institutions, fellow students, teachers, and learning resources as effectively and as intimately as students on campus. Additionally, more and more of this sort of communication and resource access will be utilized by campus-based students. Already we have seen a blurring of the boundaries in terms of administrative, teaching, and resource use. It is my contention that this blurring will be speeded up by effective use of new technologies, such that current distinctions will become irrelevant.

There is some evidence (Cox, 1985) in densely populated countries that this is happening already. Cox's observation was that tele-education (that is, education at a distance) is not much concerned with the off-campus student population, but is taking the form of extensive networking between well-established centres of learning, effectively resulting in tele-education being a campus-based activity.

A very good example of this sort of development in Australia is the Sunraysia Project, proposed by the Victorian State Working Party on Telecommunications Networking for Tertiary Education (1985). The Sunraysia Project is a satellite-based communication network linking a number of institutions, across the three sectors of post-compulsory education, to provide teaching programmes and resources to the Sunraysia College in Victoria's remote north-west. Essentially, the link will be used to provide campus-based instruction and resources, although a major extension of the Project is associated with distance education. At the same time, the network is designed to allow instruction and resources to be shared across the institutions within the network, in much the same way as Cox envisages. Within the network proposed as Stage 1 of the Project, only the Sunraysia College is geographically remote. Two of the other four institutions are in Melbourne, while the remaining two are in Geelong, an industrial city of 160,000 people located 70 kilometres from Melbourne.

The Interlink Project in Melbourne (Richardson, 1986) is another example of the use of telecommunications to provide campus-based instruction. The Project aims to explore decentralized access to vocational training, and the use of communication technologies in course presentation. It is planned to offer a number of vocational courses at six local learning centres in the outer eastern suburbs of Melbourne, using a combination of teleconferencing, facsimile and data transmission. The learning resources and instruction will emanate from a number of established TAFE colleges.

## Barriers to Using Technology in Education

As stated earlier, I believe that technology and its impact on society as described by Pawley (1973) and Toffler (1981), as well as its impact on education, has partly fuelled the growth of distance education. Distance education is congruent with the sorts of changes in our society described by these two authors. I also believe that through these technologies in their broadest sense, distance education has had an impact on educational methods in general, and will continue to be in the vanguard of educational change.

Technological change, particularly in the area of telecommunications, has the potential to change substantially the way we go about teaching, the way we go about learning, the expectations of teachers and students, and access to education.

Right now the hardware exists to enable long and regular communication between students and teachers by telephone, or by computer. The hardware also exists to enable students to access an enormous amount of learning material at home. Such resources can be print, audio, visual, and computer-aided.

The things that we lack in order to implement these technologies in education can be readily identified:

(1)  The capital investment necessary to establish a widely distributed network of broad-band carriers.

(2)  A cost structure favourable to the purchase of necessary hardware both by institutions and by students.

(3)  A favourable telecommunications tariff structure.

(4)  The availability of courseware.

(5)  Staff development for teachers and academics.

The network capital investment is a problem at present in most countries of the world. In Australia, Telecom, the telephone provider, is committed to a complete distribution of the Subscriber Trunk Dialling system within a matter of a couple of years. Telecom is also committed to the digitization of the public switched network. These developments represent considerable investment and, although broad-band coverage across the nation is not a feasible proposition in the near future, developments enabling 2 Mbit visual transmissions are close.

The digitization of the network is likely to produce a more favourable tariff structure based on signal time and time of day, rather than distance plus connect time and time of day. Use of the packet switching network, AUSTPAC, also yields very favourable tariffs at present for computer communications.

Hardware purchases necessary for institutions and for students are now more favourable. In Australia, at the end of 1984, 300,000 or around 6 per cent of Australian households owned a microcomputer. As mentioned earlier, video-cassette players were owned by around 38 per cent of Australian households at the end of 1985. At the same time, 85 per cent of households had a telephone. Clearly the community response to hardware purchases is encouraging. The institutional response is also encouraging. Government funding for purchasing and updating computing equipment in Australian institutions has been fairly readily available in the post-compulsory sector, and it is an unusual institution that lacks computing power. In other words, we have some room for optimism in that area.

In courseware availability and staff development we do not have any room for optimism at present. Courseware is only going to be developed with any sophistication if there is considerable investment in staff training, salaries, and the development of a career structure for staff training personnel. There also needs to be considerable co-operation between sectors of education, states, and individual institutions, in terms of curriculum and delivery methods. None of those components has been strongly evident, and no coherent national policy has emerged in Australia.

The same remarks can be made about staff development for teachers and academics. Certainly, there have been significant attempts to address the staff development issues in Australia, as evidenced by the report of the Australian Committee of Directors and Principals in Advanced Education (1984). But, as yet, no national coherence has emerged.

On balance it is unlikely, in spite of the barriers to convergence which exist, that the concepts and methods of distance education will remain permanently on the fringe of higher education systems. The Sunraysia and the Interlink projects are local examples in support of this view. We cannot afford to ignore, or under-utilize, methods of instruction that allow us to break away from high-cost classroom instruction, from almost total under-utilization of all educational resources at certain times of the year, and from a recurrent cost structure that is linearly related to the number of students under instruction but, in reality, has very high capital costs.

The concepts and methods of distance education will be embraced more and more by campus-based educators as they grapple with community demands in terms of student numbers and rapid response to education and training needs. Furthermore, the demand for access to education from hitherto educationally disadvantaged groups will also continue to grow, and the distance education mode can assist in meeting those demands. An additional pressure for education and training in Australia, which is typical among Western economies is that, although we have experienced higher percentages of unemployment over the past ten years, we have experienced higher percentages of employment at the same time (Cleary, 1985).

The effective use of new technologies in education will generate a momentum of its own towards the convergence of mainstream and distance education in terms of teaching methods. If I am correct in predicting that distance education will become a major force in addressing the sorts of pressures that are being experienced by educators now and will be experienced in the coming decades, then convergence of modes will be more rapid than we anticipate presently.

While the face-to-face method of instruction continues to exist in higher education (and let us sincerely hope that it always does) there will never be a total convergence of modes. There will always be opportunities for different teaching methods to exist in the campus-based situation and these should be capitalized on wherever appropriate. But there is little question that a convergence will result from the sort of teaching methods that technology can yield, and from the sorts of pressures to which education must continue to respond. Such a tendency towards convergence will also result in an educational response that is appropriate in the closing years of the twentieth century - as appropriate as a face-to-face classroom-based response was in the closing years of the nineteenth century.

# References

Australian Committee of Directors and Principals in Advanced Education (1984) *Academic Staff Development in Colleges of Advanced Education*, report of the Working Party, A.C.D.P., Braddon, A.C.T.

Cleary, M. (1985) 'Manufacturing - A Future?', *Questioning the Future*, Occasional Paper No. 1, Commission for the Future, Commonwealth of Australia, Carlton, Victoria

Cox, W.F. (1985) *Observations on Some Tele-education Trends and Developments*, Internal Report, Telecom Australia, Melbourne, Victoria

Cross, J.A. (1980) 'The Role of External Studies in Tertiary Education' in S.W. Davis, J.C. Owen and P.J. Smith (eds.), *Proceedings of the National Seminar on External Studies in Library Science*, Capricornia Institute of Advanced Education, Rockhampton

Holmberg, B. (1976) 'Academic Socialisation and Distance Study' *Epistolodidaktika*, 1, 17-23

Johnson, R. (1983) *The Provision of External Studies in Australian Higher Education*, a report prepared for the Commonwealth Tertiary Education Commission, Canberra

Kangaroo Network Bulletin (1983) PEACESAT Australia Project, Bundoora, Victoria, August 31

Laverty, J.R. (1980) 'Kevin C. Smith's "External Studies at New England - A Silver Jubilee Review 1955-1979"', *Distance Education*, 1, 2, 207-14

MacDonald, T.H. (1976) 'Problems of Teaching "Brunerian Disciplines" by External Study', *Epistolodidaktika*, 2, 74-80

McBeath, C. (1985) *Choosing National Resources for Different Learning Modes in TAFE*, TAFE National Centre for Research and Development, Adelaide

Pawley, M. (1973) *The Private Future*, Thames and Hudson, London

Richardson, L. (1986) *Technology, Access and Participation in Vocational Training*, Interlink Executive Summary, Office of the TAFE Board, Melbourne, Victoria

Romiszowski, A.J. (1981) *Designing Instructional Systems*, Kogan Page, London

Rumble, G. and Keegan, D. (1982) 'Distance Teaching at University Level', in G. Rumble and K. Harry (eds.), *The Distance Teaching Universities*, Croom Helm, London

Smith, K.C. (1979) *External Studies at New England: A Silver Jubilee Review* 1955-1979, University of New England,

Armidale, N.S.W.

Toffler, A. (1981) *The Third Wave*, Pan Books, London

Victorian State Working Party on Telecommunications Networking for Tertiary Education (1985) *The Sunraysia Project*, Sunraysia College of TAFE, Mildura, N.S.W.

**Peter J. Smith**, BPsych(Hons) DipEd *W.Aust.*, GradDipAdmin *W.A.I.T.*, MEdAdmin *U.N.E.*, MAPsS

Head,
Learning Resource Centre,
The Gordon Technical College,
Australia

Chapter Three

BRIDGING THE TECHNOLOGY-PEDAGOGY GAP

James W. Hall

Previously I have referred to telecommunications in the university as 'the dragon in academia'. This dragon has slithered out of its cave from time to time, has crept up to the walls of the university with a considerable belching of smoke (but not very much fire), has made a brief and threatening attack, and, after being thrown a few sacrificial bodies, has retreated to its lair without seriously discommoding anyone, least of all, students. Generally speaking, the impact on higher education of the telecommunication dragon, with its gnarled old twin horns of radio and video, has been rather innocuous. More recently the old dragon has teamed with a second, the microprocessor dragon, and, in tandem, these two are assaulting the fortified towers of the university again. This time there appears to be more fire than smoke.

These new protean dragons come in a more formidable shape than before. Their newest features are the 256K microchip; the digital TV set with split-screen, immediate recall, and video recording; the laser video-disc with its 54,000 frame storage and instant retrieval capability; and the microwave dish with the ability to snatch multiple signals from distant satellites. As if this is not enough, these new dragons are capable of rapid metamorphosis. They constantly assume new dimensions and capabilities, which confuses academia mightily. Probably it is time for the university to try to domesticate the telecommunication dragons, to bring them fully within the university's walls, and to harness their considerable energies in its enterprise. Low-cost electronic hardware is now available, data bases and programmed educational course materials are increasingly accessible, and reception of information can now be linked to interactive teaching. With these capabilities, the so-called 'electronic university' becomes technologically feasible, bringing learning via the distance education mode.

Yet technological feasibility is not enough. A fundamental question still requires an answer. Can existing organizational structures within universities accommodate these varied technologies, or are new structures required before significant and high-quality use of technological breakthroughs in teaching and learning is possible?

It is my judgement that if significant, large-scale use of telecommunications technology is to be effective, new organizational structures are required within universities. It seems inescapable to conclude that, in a campus-based setting, where teaching occurs in a classroom, there is a rather circumscribed future for telecommunications technology. Students like to participate in a classroom setting. They enjoy discussing ideas and issues with fellow students. Given the competition of an effective teacher and a stimulating group of students, this technology finishes a very poor third. As an adjunct to classroom instruction, some telecommunications devices can function as a solid drill sergeant. Such technology-driven drills can help students in the library or the learning resources centre. Campus-based students pursuing such subjects as engineering, language, music, graphics, and certain forms of problem-solving do benefit from extra drill and computation via the computer. However, the principal method of instruction remains the face-to-face lecture with direct access to the teacher. For campus-based students, telecommunications technology will have a useful, but not revolutionary impact on pedagogy.

On the other hand, courses offered to students who are unable to study on a campus offer a magnificent opportunity for the use of such technology. These students cannot sit in a classroom at the foot of a teacher. These students cannot come to resource centres for drill via computer or video-cassette. For these students the convenience, flexibility and pedagogy of telecommunications technology are not merely useful supplements, but are essential to their ability to study at all.

## Technology and Effective Learning

Unfortunately, availability of telecommunications technology does not automatically ensure effective learning. Experience shows an alarming and predictable gap in student engagement and persistence. I choose to call this the **technology-pedagogy gap**. Few academics have thought very much about how to teach distance education students, and in most cases the solution is pedestrian: either to transplant the classroom to a remote location, or to offer written forms of campus-based lectures. Both solutions have been proven to be of limited effectiveness in maintaining student motivation and persistence. With few exceptions, existing university teaching methods and structures are unprepared to exploit the new technologies effectively.

Campus-based organizational structures have been unable to conceptualize and deliver effective instruction to distance education students. There are, of course, a few examples of effective use of the distance education mode using print materials, occasionally enhanced by television. But most often these efforts merely duplicate campus-based teaching methods. And in any case the organizational structures of the university ensure that these 'deviant' teaching methods are not permitted to become central and threatening to mainstream teaching methods. My observations should not be taken as a criticism of campus-based structures. These function well, have provided an excellent education for many students, and will undoubtedly continue to do so. However, the successful employment of telecommunications technology, for that very large group of distance education students who have no other way to study, requires new methods of organization.

Planning for telecommunications in the service of distance education students ought not to begin with the iconoclastic notion that the university of the present is outdated, irrelevant and ineffective. Rather, it should begin with the assumption that the university, with its great strengths and enduring values, can be adjusted organizationally and structurally, so that the qualitative essentials of a great university - academics, scholarly and research resources, and pedagogy - can be extended to reach students not now served. One major reason that electronic media and the university have often failed to connect with each other is that the theoreticians and practitioners of each seriously misunderstand one another. Telecommunications holds the promise not only to fulfil the older notions of university extension, but also to bring to distance education students that quality of education associated with campus-based teaching at its best. Such quality will be possible because, for the first time, all the resources of the university can be made available to distance education students.

In this morphism, the university campus will emphasize its role as a dynamic intellectual centre wherein new knowledge and ideas are generated. Building on these traditional strengths, the university can design and support a variety of pedagogies and delivery methods which bring the university to the students, whether it be in the home, the workplace, the library, or other location.

The revolution in telecommunications has the potential to increase access to learning. Knowledge can be carried into the most isolated localities and into basic social institutions and situations. **But such access to knowledge does not in itself produce a learning situation: that state in which the learner is fully active.** Nor does it solve the problem of how new information and knowledge transmitted electronically will interact with the other basic forms of social communication that bind communities together - encounters at work, word of mouth among neighbours, conversations in families. If new access and new types of organization are to emerge, we must focus as much on reception as on 'packaging' of the media.

Perhaps the central difficulty in all this is what one might call the illusion of access. It is true that telecommunications reduces distance to negligible proportions. The simple act of pushing a button brings messages to students quickly and effortlessly, but perhaps it is this seeming ease that produces a

47

characteristic state of relaxation, of passivity in the presence of media. It is all done for us, though we maintain the fiction of control through our power to change the channel or flip a switch. Consequently educators who use telecommunications must stimulate behaviour, encourage a posture and practice for learning that is active, alert, serious. Only in this way can it bring genuine and full access. Planners need to consider a supporting organizational structure which can stimulate an inward and critical involvement on the part of students that leads to questioning and dialogue.

It is also misperception about the meaning and character of higher education itself that accounts for many of the limitations of distance education learning. Methods of instruction, including correspondence, television, and computer-assisted courses prove highly efficient in helping students address such fundamental aspects of learning as the acquisition of **knowledge** and **communication skills**. But while these are the essential broad bases for a solid higher education, they do not in themselves enable students to attain those higher skills and abilities which must characterize a high quality baccalaureate. These higher intellectual and personal dimensions have seldom been treated systematically by distance educators and, indeed, they are achieved only occasionally by the most effective campus-based teachers. Nonetheless, if distance education is to achieve recognized high quality, it must strive to achieve an educational potential best expressed by the concept displayed in Figure 3.1.

It is not enough to convey facts and develop students' communication skills. Rather analysis, synthesis, application and, finally, valuation or judgement are the hallmarks of the educated person. It is these higher intellectual achievements, characteristic of a truly **higher** education, that the designers of educational software have usually neglected.

Today, emerging interactive telecommunications hold high promise to accommodate teaching and learning pedagogies which nurture and elicit such advanced skills and abilities from students. But those who create these educational pedagogies will need to be guided by well-defined concepts of what higher learning is really about, and how it can be stimulated. The best

**Figure 3.1:** Pyramid of the Educated Person

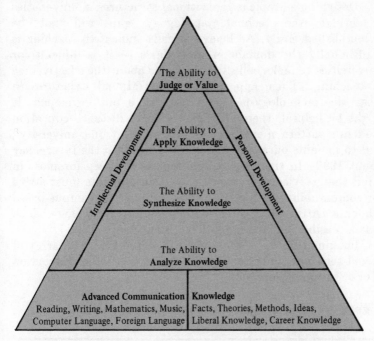

Source:   James W. Hall with Barbara L. Kevles (1982) 'A
          Model College Education: From an Atraditional
          Viewpoint', *In Opposition to Core Curriculum;
          Alternative Models for Undergraduate Education*,
          James W. Hall, Ed., with Barbara L. Kevles,
          Greenwood Press, Westport, Ct., p. 205.

teachers, always few in number, have known how to do
precisely that. Can we capture those concepts, those
techniques for advanced learning, and realize them in distance
education? This is the real challenge for educators who would
use telecommunications for higher education. This is the
technology-pedagogy gap which must be overcome if the use of
telecommunications in serving distance education students is
to be effective.

## Designing Organizational Structures

Designing suitable organizational structures in universities to bridge the technology-pedagogy gap will not be accomplished easily. As I have already indicated, teaching is traditionally the domain of individuals so it is difficult for universities to make collective decisions about the effectiveness of teaching. Thus, appropriate organizational structures to close the technology-pedagogy gap have not developed. It might be helpful, therefore, to consider a distance education student's pattern of engagement with an 'electronic university', and to imagine ourselves just a few years into the future, say about 1990. In this speculation, we should keep foremost in mind that service to distance education students must strive for comparability with services now available to campus-based students. After all, it is telecommunications technology which makes feasible our contemplation of such comparability.

Imagine that our 1990 student is seated before an array of linked telecommunications media called the Higher Education Work Station (Figure 3.2).

**Figure 3.2:** Higher Education Work Station (HEWS)

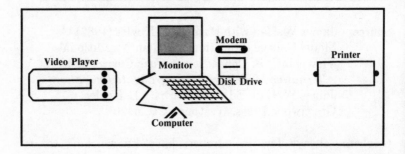

This work station, which can be found in North America, in most community libraries, in many governmental and postal offices, and in some small places of corporate business, is also replicated at modest cost in many homes. Such a work station is now sufficiently ubiquitous to allow its use by virtually every distance education student, including those who are handicapped, incarcerated, or impecunious.

Accessibility through HEWS, more than anything else, accounts for the fact that the university now recognizes that distance education students are the regular and essential audience for all university programmes, not merely, as in previous years, a handful of exotics to be served through a number of profitable 'special programmes'. Without labouring the point, the range of students who are now served extends to any person who can be linked to the network, and is virtually unlimited as to place and time of study.

These changes did not happen without some significant modifications in the way the university operated. First the academics had to understand that the technology-pedagogy gap was not something which might be bridged by simple tinkering. The academics of the 'electronic university' of 1990 found that a thoroughgoing reconceptualization of the entire university organizational structure was required to adequately serve distance education students. To illustrate this I will comment on three aspects of the organization of universities that had to be reconsidered. These aspects are: (1) pre-enrolment counselling; (2) the availability of hardware and software for communication; (3) the way in which teachers interact with students.

(1) How prospective students gain sufficient information to apply for matriculation is less important to our discussion than the immediate availability of detailed, interactive pre-enrolment counselling which leads students to make informed course choices within a larger set of educational goals. How does real planning and counselling occur?

Working at HEWS, the student's first contact with the university is a battery of interactive questions which helps the student to project, within a very short time, a set of goals and tentative courses. The student is then able to forward personal

51

inquiries to individual departments via electronic mail and to make a preliminary judgement about course registration. The student is also able to draw on such materials as standard catalogue descriptions or the student electronic newspaper displaying the latest 'inside' information on course effectiveness.

In this way, the student's interests, achievements and capabilities are quickly assessed, and a sequence of interactive discussions with specially trained advisers is completed. The important thing to note here is that the electronic dialogue is not limited to a student interacting with a machine, programmed to anticipate a wide range of possible questions. In addition to valuable counselling software, the indispensable ingredient is access to individuals - teachers, advisers, assistants - who can respond through electronic mail. The combination of sophisticated diagnostic tools and responsible counselling is actually an improvement on previous, largely serendipitous, approaches to pre-enrolment counselling.

While curricula for distance education students often focused only on the lower levels of learning, for example, basic information and communication skills, telecommunications and advanced software now offer improved tools for building into the instructional design a potential for achievement of higher level intellectual skills. Moreover, in our vision of the 'electronic university' of 1990, the range of courses is now large and their nature is interactive because of rapid advances in educational software. The greater number of courses is possible because they are now available from many sources and traditional textbook publishers engage academics to create third-generation software for the superb hardware which is now available. Also, since physical space does not limit the ability of students to enrol in a course, increased numbers of otherwise qualified students can be admitted to 'places'. Thus, for all practical purposes, the differences between campus-based and distance education students are virtually gone.

(2) I will now comment on the specific telecommunications technologies which provide adequate communication and delivery of education, and the software necessary to carry out all of the various university interactions with students.

Above we imagined a student of the future seated before an impressive array of technology, called HEWS. In fact the technology for HEWS was available in 1985, but its cost was too high for most students; the software was still too primitive; and the transmission of data was far too slow. Moreover, the university in 1985 had not yet determined how to use this educational delivery and communication tool effectively.

Then came several key improvements with startling rapidity. First, the cost of purchasing good quality, high capacity equipment came within range of most organizations and many households. Second, the spread of digital transmission over regional communication networks dramatically increased the speed and quantity of real time communication, and at reasonable cost.

Although the particular design of the 1990s' work station varies, it typically features the linkage of a computer and terminal with large memory, two disk drives, a video-disc and tape player, and a network. Its graphic reproduction capability is far superior to the earlier form, for picture transmission is easily achieved by a mounted video-camera. Transmission speeds now permit rapid photo-communication. Translation via modem to analog form is no longer necessary. All of this is essential to the highly interactive instructional software and new university organizational structures.

(3) How do teachers support learning by providing feedback and evaluation of student performance, and how do they guide and facilitate access to resources such as books, guides, and data bases? This was perhaps the most difficult challenge for the teachers in the 1990s' 'electronic university'. Their time-honoured methods of lecturing to students about their latest research findings and sending students to the library for further study are simply not possible for distance education students. Lectures are now recorded on video and are available to be downloaded from a central data bank to the student's work station at any convenient time. The same is true for bibliographies, printed materials, and a wide variety of data bases and analytical systems software. Students pursue most of their study independently, but are expected to discuss key concepts and questions with mentor-teachers by electronic

53

mail. Papers written by students and responses from mentors are also transmitted electronically and can be reviewed by each party at a convenient time.

These new organizational structures have changed the role of many academics. Additionally, HEWS has brought an end to the previous calendar of terms or semesters with fixed course schedules, and has been highly popular with students everywhere.

These three areas which are crucial in bridging the technology-pedagogy gap for the 'electronic university' in 1990 are, of course, only suggestive and so risk trivializing enormous complexity and conflict. But I am persuaded that the distance education student will not be served adequately by the telecommunications technologies at hand until a thoroughgoing restructuring of universities occurs.

## Technological Infrastructure

It is clear that the 'electronic university' described above requires an advanced and costly national technological infrastructure and this leads me to a series of concluding observations which are sobering.

In the developed nations of the world, the existence of widespread campus-based educational opportunities beyond the compulsory schooling level tends to minimize the social and political demand for distance education. Conversely, in nations which are not so developed economically, universities are often limited to an elite core of students. In these nations, most of the available government support for education has funded a massive expansion of elementary and secondary education, aiming primarily for widespread competency in literacy and technical/vocational subjects. But today, as increasingly large numbers of students complete this education, the demand for higher education is considerable. One result has been substantial political pressure for governments to establish distance education universities which can accommodate large numbers of students while minimizing the need to invest in brick and mortar campuses. Indeed, today **10 million** students are enrolled in such universities across the world. These universities would seem to be the great testing area for the use of telecommunications technology in education.

The most intriguing opportunities for intensive and widespread use of such technology are likely to be found in the less economically developed nations where the demands for higher education are very great and the resources modest. It is in such nations as Nigeria, Thailand, China, and Pakistan where telecommunications **could** have a remarkable impact in extending education to people unable to study on a campus.

But this presents a paradox: such technology requires sophisticated national telecommunications infrastructures. Ironically those nations which have the necessary telecommunications and postal infrastructures are precisely those nations in which the needs of students are met most fully by campus-based education. Conversely, those nations which most need distance education to reach their burgeoning and geographically widespread populations, lack the necessary national telecommunications infrastructures. This paradox contributes to a situation in which most of our experience regarding the merits or weaknesses of technology comes from those who have the least real need to use it. My point here is that we do not get a truly accurate picture of the potential value of telecommunications technology. We have primarily only the pedagogical experiences and opinions of those faculties for whom it is at best a supplementary, wholly optional, medium for study.

In the economically developed nations which have the technological capability, there is an insufficient mass of students who will actually use elaborate telecommunications systems. Governments in these nations do not support systems for use of telecommunications technology in education with public funds because no strong political constituency exists for whom these alternate systems of higher education are absolutely essential.

So the telecommunications dragons will require a lot more time to domesticate, and quite a few more bodies are likely to be seared by the dragons' fire before we carefully channel their terrible and terrific force toward the betterment of education.

Working now to overcome the technology-pedagogy gap can do much to bring that day closer.

**James W. Hall**, PhD *Penn.*

President and Professor of Social Sciences
Empire State College
State University of New York
U.S.A.

Chapter Four

# DISTANCE EDUCATION IN KENYA: A THIRD WORLD VIEW

Barbara Matiru

In recent years there has been an upsurge in distance education programmes world-wide. Kenya is no exception. Distance education is essential if the government is to meet its commitments to teacher training, secondary education and adult literacy: existing campuses cannot accommodate the large numbers of people who are currently in need of education. This need is reflected in the increasing number of government-sponsored distance education programmes and in the fact that the Institute of Adult Studies of the University of Nariobi has been elevated to the College of Adult and Distance Education.

The College now enrols over 9000 students and it has just launched a distance education degree programme. The fact that over 8000 potential students applied for the 600 places that were available initially in this programme, exemplifies the demand for distance education.

Other government institutions such as the Co-operative College of Kenya, the Kenya Institute of Education, Tom Mboya Labour College and Moi Polytechnic also offer courses at a distance. In addition, some private and international organizations, including the African Medical Research Foundation, the Hadley School for the Blind and the African Institute for Economic and Social Development, have ventured into the field.

## Reasons for the Growth in Distance Education in Kenya

Kenya made enormous achievements in education soon after Independence in 1963, with a large increase in the number of children attending school. In the three-year period from 1963, the number of pupils enrolled in primary schools increased from 890,000 to 1,600,000. This increase resulted from a growing public demand for education, an enlarged school age population and the government's commitment to make education accessible to more and more Kenyans.

The main reason for the growth of distance education in Kenya is that the mainstream educational system is unable to cater for the great number of people who now want to further their education. This is so especially in the areas of initial teacher training and upgrading, secondary education, and business studies.

As is the case in many Western countries, there is a need for inservice training which cannot be met by campus-based education. Therefore, institutions in Kenya entered the field of distance education to supplement campus-based educational efforts.

The Correspondence Course Unit of the College of Adult and Distance Education, at the University of Nairobi, was established in 1967 to meet the urgent need to upgrade the qualifications of primary school teachers. At that time Kenya had a large number of teachers who had only a primary school education themselves, with two years of professional training. Academically these teachers were hardly more schooled than the children in upper primary school classes. The programme offered by the Correspondence Course Unit was to provide two years of secondary education leading to the Kenya Junior Seondary Examination. The programme was not meant to train teachers in classroom methodology but to improve their academic knowledge, with the hope that after receiving their training, the teachers would, in turn, improve the quality of education in primary schools.

In 1969 a second programme was started concurrently with the Kenya Junior Secondary Examination course. Jointly with

58

the Kenya Institute of Education, the Correspondence Course Unit began a programme aimed at upgrading teachers who had no professional training at all. These teachers either did not have a full primary education or had failed the examination at the end of primary school.

The number of children enrolled in primary schools reached a critical peak in 1974 when the government announced the elimination of school fees for levels one through to four. Each year thereafter, the remaining levels had fees removed and consequently enrolments increased.

During the period 1968-1979 the primary school teaching force grew by 142 per cent from 38,300 to 92,800. By 1981 the number of teachers had increased to 110,000.

The Fifth Development Plan for Kenya launched a full eight-year basic education programme, commencing in 1985, as the first phase in the introduction of the 8-4-4 system of education (eight years of primary education, four years of secondary education and four years of university education). An additional 22,500 untrained teachers were recruited that year. This resulted in over 50,000 untrained primary school teachers unevenly distributed around the country.

In addition to training primary school teachers, the need to train teachers for the Department of Adult Education had become apparent in 1979 when a campaign to irradicate illiteracy in Kenya was started. The government put emphasis on this area because it considered a lack of education and the inability to read and write as one of the three national enemies - the others being poverty, and disease - which must be dealt with before individual and national development could take place. A survey carried out in 1980-1981 found that 55.9 per cent of the population aged fifteen years and over in rural areas were illiterate, and 52 per cent of the total population had no schooling. Therefore the Department of Adult Education recruited an additional 3000 literacy teachers to help teach some 350,000 adult students. The most suitable method for training these new teachers was by means of distance education because they could remain on the job while they were being trained. The College of Adult and Distance Education was requested to design and run such a programme.

In 1985 the Correspondence Course Unit of the College of Adult and Distance Education became the School of Distance Studies. It now offers two preparatory courses, a foundation course in adult education, a teacher inservice course and commercial courses. Further courses are under development in agriculture, accounting and business.

At the same time as the School of Distance Studies was formed, the Faculty of External Degree Studies was incorporated into the College of Adult and Distance Education. The urgent need for the Faculty of External Degree Studies is evident from the fact that in 1986 approximately 5000 students qualified to enter university, yet despite great efforts by the government to establish new universities, only about 2500 new places were available. Because the demand for higher education is increasing, this shortfall in places available will certainly increase during the coming years.

Institutions in Kenya which offer programmes in the distance education mode are thus supplementing campus-based educational facilities in an attempt to respond to demand caused by:

(1) The high level of illiteracy amongst the adult population.

(2) The ever increasing numbers of school and university enrolments as a result of high population growth.

(3) The acute shortage of qualified manpower.

(4) A shortage of qualified teachers and trainers.

## Methods of Teaching at a Distance

Almost all distance education programmes in Kenya consist of the following components:

(1) Printed materials which consist of study guides and textbooks.

(2) Radio broadcasts or audio-cassettes which give explanations additional to the printed materials.

(3) Occasional face-to-face teaching during residential sessions.

(4) Guides and timetables for the radio broadcasts.

Students are encouraged to be self-disciplined in choosing a suitable number of courses and in setting themselves a reasonable time to complete their studies. They are advised when to sit for examinations and are given assistance to plan a convenient individual timetable that will allow them to include their studies as part of their everyday life. Course materials are carefully checked before they are sent out. Tutors are instructed to mark assignments strictly but always to give helpful comments. Students may write to tutors on any problem related to the content of their programme.

To be able to offer distance education programmes, institutions require efficient organizational infrastructures. Most distance education departments are headed by a director and have a regular full-time staff of tutors to look after the printed materials, a radio tutor, a course editor, a counsellor, and administrative and clerical personnel. They draw upon the services of school teachers as well as university and college lecturers as part-time course writers and assignment markers. Production sections are equipped with modern typing, printing, duplicating and binding facilities. There are registration, mailing, records and stores sections where enrolment forms, printed materials, and assignments are processed. Usually there are self-contained recording and production studios for preparing radio broadcasts or audio-cassettes and a small laboratory which sends out science kits.

## The Inservice Course for Untrained Primary School Teachers

The Inservice Course for Primary School Teachers offered by the School of Distance Studies is a good example of how a distance education course is organized in Kenya, of the kinds of students who undertake distance education courses and of the problems which they encounter in their studies. The course is intended for untrained primary school teachers who have been teaching for a minimum of three years. The students are categorized P1, P2, or P3 according to their qualifications at the time they enter the course. The entry qualification of P1 students is seven years of primary plus four years of secondary education; for P2 students, seven years of primary plus two years of secondary education; and, for P3 students, seven years of primary education.

Students are required to study twelve subjects. To be awarded a P1, P2 or P3 Teacher's Certificate students must pass written examinations in these subjects. There are also written assignments and assessment of practical teaching skills.

The course has three components: printed materials, radio broadcasts and residential sessions. The School of Distance Studies produces a series of six study guides for each subject. The study guides cover the theoretical aspects of the subject. During the residential sessions, students are taught the practical aspects of the subject by full-time College tutors. The Educational Media Service of the Kenya Institute of Education produces the radio broadcasts which teach topics not covered by either of the other components. There is continuous assessment of the printed materials based on the assignments that are part of every subject.

During the residential sessions, an evaluation team consisting of staff from the Educational Media Service, the School of Distance Studies and the Inspectorate of the Ministry of Education, Science and Technology visits the students. The aim of these visits is to help students with problems that they find in the printed materials or in the radio broadcasts. The staff from the Inspectorate check to see that the students are properly taught in residence, and that they are adequately supervised and graded in their practical teaching sessions.

## Characteristics of Students in the Inservice Course

A knowledge of the characteristics of the students enrolled in the Inservice Course is important, because factors such as age and marital status are presumed to influence a student's approach to distance studies. A survey of the Inservice Course for Primary School Teachers which was carried out in 1985 is reported in full in Matiru and Kamau (1985). Results of the survey revealed that the students taking this course had the following characteristics.

**Age.** The students' ages ranged between 20 and 49 years. Many of them left school quite a number of years ago, so returning to study might not have been easy.

The majority of P3 students were between 30 and 34 years whereas the majority of P1 and P2 students were between 25 and 34 years. The majority of P1s and P2s between the ages of 20 and 24 years were female. On the other hand, the majority of P3s of the same age were males. There were no female P1 and P2 students over the age of 35 years.

**Teaching Experience.** The ages of students had a direct bearing on the number of years they had taught.

The majority of P1 and P2 male and female students and P3 female students had taught for between 6-10 years without receiving any form of training. Many had taught 11-15 years and a few of the P2 and P3s for as many as 16-25 years.

According to Kenyan government policy, untrained teachers should receive professional training after serving for three years. So the fact that untrained teachers have been teaching for over ten years seems rather unfortunate. The Inservice Course is providing an opportunity for such teachers to receive a professional qualification which they would not have obtained otherwise.

Although the P3s formed the greatest number who had taught for over ten years (16 per cent males and 27 per cent females) the majority of the P3s (66 per cent males and 21 per cent females) had taught for five years or less. This means that this group has the greatest number of young, inexperienced students (particularly males) as well as the greatest number of old and experienced ones. Perhaps this is one of the factors which accounts for the P3 group having the greatest difficulties with the course.

**Marital Status.** Eighty-six per cent of the students were married (87 per cent males and 85 per cent females) and were raising families. This meant they had extra responsibilities which reduced the amount of time they could spend on their studies. Many of the females were nursing mothers who had to combine their employment and studies with taking care of their young families and at the same time breast-feeding their baby. Also many were often the only salaried members of a larger extended family and so had a great responsibility to these relatives.·

### General Problems with the Inservice Course

The general problems encountered by students studying at a distance in Kenya can be exemplified by the students enrolled in the Inservice Course for Primary School Teachers. The results of the Matiru and Kamau (1985) survey of this course once again forms the basis for the following discussion.

**The Printed Materials Component.** Thirty-four per cent of the students said that the printed materials were not always clear. Perhaps this is due to the fact that most subjects depend on a sound knowledge of the language of instruction - either English or Kiswahili, neither of which is the mother tongue of over 90 per cent of the students.

Students who indicated that the materials were not clear were asked to give reasons. They said that the study guides were too difficult because the language was difficult and the illustrations and diagrams were difficult to understand. In all cases, males expressed slightly more concern about these difficulties than did females.

In addition, some students said that the terms used were difficult; written assignments asked questions which could not be answered from the study guide; often pages were missing or mixed up in the study guides; study guides were delayed and so it was not easy to keep to a logical sequence of study; there were too many units making up each subject and they were too long; materials should be written specifically for the P1, P2 and P3 groups of students; students were directed to reference books that were not available; there was a lack of diagrams in mathematics.

Although students indicated that they had problems with difficult language and content in the study guides, over 70 per cent reported that they were able to complete all the self-tests and self-assessment questions. Difficult as the course may be, the majority of students are, however, determined to do their studies. The thirteen tutors who were also interviewed for the survey confirmed some of the statements made by the students.

The problem of the clarity of study materials could have been identified earlier if the printed materials had been pre-tested. Unfortunately, the School of Distance Studies was given no time in which to develop, pre-test and then improve the course materials. As is usual in a developing country, the course was needed so urgently that it was launched before much of the material had been written.

**Efficiency of the Delivery of the Printed Materials.** Students were asked to indicate if they received the printed materials on time. Thirty-eight per cent reported that they did not. There was little difference between what was reported by students living in the developed and undeveloped regions of Kenya; that is, those areas with good road networks and a reliable postal service and those with few roads and limited postal service. Therefore, road networks and postal services were not a major cause of delays. The writing, production and marking processes at the School of Distance Studies must, therefore, constitute the major delay. It is known that sometimes there is no money to buy materials such as paper for printing the study guides and a whole month may be wasted waiting for money from the Treasury to buy paper and sometimes stamps.

Students who said that they received their materials late also said that they could not keep a logical sequence of the topics taught in each subject due to the long time that elapsed before they got the next study guide. Delay, therefore, hindered some students from realizing systematic progress in their studies.

Of the thirteen tutors interviewed for the survey, six said that students had complained to them about receiving their printed materials late. Because of that delay, students had not covered the theory in these subjects. As a result, when they went to the residential session to study the practical aspects of the course, most of them could not understand the content because they lacked the theoretical background. The administrators of the Inservice Course for Primary School Teachers said that the delay in the dispatch of study guides and marked assignments was interfering with the general progress of the entire course.

It was encouraging to note, however, that when the students did get their materials, 72 per cent said they got the correct ones. This finding suggests that the sorting and packaging of materials to be mailed is done fairly efficiently.

**Tutoring and Assignment Marking.** Students were asked to indicate whether their tutors were helpful. Results varied from subject to subject but overall 56.86 per cent of students found tutors to be very helpful or helpful, 11.92 per cent found them unhelpful and 31.18 per cent gave no response. The reasons the students gave for their tutors not being helpful were that they did not indicate how to correct mistakes, did not comment on work achievement, and criticized the students.

The students also complained that cover sheets and envelopes were not provided for the assignments and that the work was not returned promptly. Delays in the return of assignments and negative comments were very discouraging for the students because they did not receive any immediate help apart from that given by the tutors when marking assignments.

**The Radio Component.** In some cases the radio broadcasts

complemented the material in the study guides. In other cases certain topics were covered only by the radio component. It was, therefore, imperative that students listen to all the radio broadcasts. It was disappointing to find that only 32 per cent of students listened to the radio regularly and that 35 per cent listened only occasionally. The P1 group listened to the radio more often than the other categories. This factor probably contributed to their better performance. The reasons students gave for not listening to the radio broadcasts were poor reception; that 3.30 p.m. is an unsuitable time; that they lacked time to listen; and that they had no radio.

Also many of the students were still teaching their own classes at the time of the radio broadcasts; many had staff meetings or games to supervise at the time; poor weather frequently interrupted the reception; and, in quite a few cases, headmasters took the school radio home. A number of students had long distances to walk home (eighteen kilometres or more) and so could not stay at their school to listen to the radio broadcasts. Forty-five per cent said they would prefer to listen to the radio broadcasts later in the day.

It was interesting to find that of those who listened to the radio, 52 per cent did so alone and 21 per cent did so with other students on the course. More males than females listened with others. Thirty-five per cent listened to the radio at school while another 35 per cent listened to it at home. Only 9 per cent had to listen in someone else's house.

When they were listening to the radio, 73 per cent said they made notes. Sixty-eight per cent of these students said that the radio broadcasts were helpful. They reported the radio broadcasts were useful in improving subject knowledge; providing encouragement; providing additional explanations; and enabling correction of mistakes.

Again, it was the P1 group who found the radio broadcasts most useful, especially as far as additional explanations were concerned. More females than males found that the radio helped them to understand better (22 per cent versus 18 per cent) and that it gave useful explanations (65 per cent versus 57 per cent). Quite a few students (19 per cent) reported that they found the pace of the radio component too fast.

In commenting on the radio component, administrators of the Inservice Course for Primary School Teachers said the radio guides and timetables were often delayed, making it impossible for students to follow the broadcasts systematically. They agreed that the scheduling of the broadcasts was inconvenient for a number of students and that poor radio reception often made the broadcasts impossible to follow.

**The Residential Component.** As far as the residential component of the course was concerned, the administrators said that the students found it difficult to pay the fee required. Another difficulty was that nursing mothers were unable to concentrate on their studies or do homework in the evening because they were busy minding their babies. Also, nursing mothers brought 'ayahs' (child nurses) to mind their babies and this arrangement was a drain on finances as the 'ayahs' were not budgeted for. It was reported that tutors and course directors were often disgruntled because they were underpaid for running the residential component. These factors at times disrupted efficient and concentrated learning and teaching in the residential sessions.

**The Relation Between Course Components.** Students were asked whether the printed materials and radio broadcasts prepared them for the residential component. Thirty-three per cent felt they were very adequately prepared and 34 per cent said they were adequately prepared. All groups held similar views on this issue. In addition, about 60 per cent thought that the study guides, the radio broadcasts and the residential sessions together covered each subject adequately.

The administrators of the Inservice Course for Primary School Teachers made the following comments concerning the harmony of the three components. Marks obtained in assignments did not agree with marks given to students during the residential sessions. Assignment marks were higher than those obtained by the same students during the face-to-face residential and practical sessions. Therefore, it was thought that students might be collaborating in doing their assignments, since it is not possible for the School of Distance

Studies to monitor whether students honestly did work on their own or whether they sought help from others.

**Practical Difficulties in Studying at a Distance.** The students encountered a number of problems in studying at a distance. These included insufficient light. In a developing country such as Kenya, 25 per cent of the students do not have sufficient light by which to study. Too much noise; family illness; the need to nurse babies and/or look after children; too much household work; and an uncooperative spouse were also sources of practical difficulty for students.

Females had more personal and family problems which directly interfered with their studies. Forty-six per cent were burdened with too much household work and 24 per cent were busy looking after children.

These problems had a direct bearing on the times when males and females could study. More males could study immediately after school (26 per cent) as compared to females, many of whom (30 per cent) said that they could only study between 9 p.m. and midnight. Also 40 per cent of the males said that they usually studied between 7 and 9 p.m. whereas fewer females said they did so at that time. This may be due to the fact that the females were busy looking after children and were involved in other household chores at these times.

When asked to state other problems that hinder their studies, a number of students said that the teaching load of their job was too heavy because schools were understaffed and that after school hours they were busy with preparations for the next day or with correcting their pupils' work. These findings were corroborated by the thirteen course tutors. The tutors said that the majority of students, especially females, complained of lack of time to concentrate on their printed materials.

Most of the students devoted only one or two hours a day to their studies, two or three days per week. This is most likely because of their own heavy teaching load at work and their personal commitments at home and in the community.

**Positive Comments on the Course.** Apart from preparing

them for the Teacher's Certificate examination, students surveyed in 1985 felt that the course also prepared them in other ways to be better teachers. It is interesting to note that an average of 72 per cent of the students thought that the course improved their teaching. They thought that it built their confidence in the classroom (49 per cent), improved their knowledge of the different teaching subjects (44 per cent), and their language (39 per cent). The P1 group seemed to find the course more useful than the other categories. There was no measurable difference between male and female responses. It was also interesting that 26 per cent of students reported that they shared their course materials with others who were not enrolled in the course. These included fellow teachers, family members, friends, and school children.

When asked to give other reasons why they found the course useful, students stated that it helped to correct their mistakes after many years of teaching without any training; taught them approaches to classroom teaching; made them discover they were not very far from being a good teacher; improved class management; saved them from constantly running to trained teachers for help; gained them respect from their friends and colleagues; and encouraged them to aim for higher education.

## Restraints and Benefits of Distance Education in Kenya

### Restraints

Unfortunately nations like Kenya, which most need systems of telecommunications technology to teach their growing and geographically scattered populations, lack the necessary infrastructure. At present, distance education teaching methods in Kenya are limited to printed materials, the radio and the occasional use of audio-cassette tapes. Very few people in Kenya own a television and those who do, live mainly in the cities where access to campus-based education is easier. Even where the radio is used to support distance education programmes, it does not reach everyone: there are still pockets of the country where the reception is very poor. Quite a number of people still do not own a radio and even if they do, cannot, at times, afford to buy batteries or get their radios repaired. On top of that, there are only two radio channels and all the educational programmes fight for prime time, together with popular entertainment and news features. Very few students have cassette players and when these are provided to institutions they quickly fall into disrepair or disappear into private homes. There has been no effort to use the telephone since it is too expensive and the lines are often very unclear.

## Benefits

Over the last twenty years, distance educators in Kenya have been able to use some technology on a modest scale to reach a large number of students. These students are, in fact, much better off than many of their campus-based colleagues who lack textbooks and printed materials and who never have the opportunity to carry out science experiments or listen to the radio or to audio-cassettes. Moreover, by using the same staff who teach in the colleges and universities, distance education is able to improve on what goes on in those institutions. Course writers, assignment writers and tutors are given training in the use of appropriate methods for distance education students and often their campus-based teaching is improved. This is evident in the materials they prepare and the counselling they give to campus-based students.

Because face-to-face interaction is not a part of presenting the basic information in distance education, those who prepare the materials make a greater effort to stimulate and encourage learning in a way that is active, alert and serious. Thus distance education students are given an opportunity to apply their knowledge in a practical way and to synthesize and analyse it. This does not always happen in the campus-based classroom or lecture hall.

Evidence of the quality of distance education materials is shown in the fact that the materials prepared for the Inservice

71

Course for Primary School Teachers are now being widely used by teachers in campus-based colleges for their preservice courses. In the past, the Kenya Junior Secondary Examination and, at present, the Kenya Certificate of Education preparatory course materials are also in great demand by school teachers who want to use them to prepare candidates for the government examinations.

Distance education in Kenya is fulfilling its intended purpose by enabling people to have access to an education they might otherwise not have had. Professional inservice training is provided to teachers and business people. Also youth and adults have the opportunity to acquire a secondary school and university education. In addition, the programmes are not a drain on the small pool of trained workers because the students can continue in employment while upgrading their qualifications.

Despite its constraints, distance education has a great potential in a developing country like Kenya because it helps to overcome the shortage of classrooms, inadequate numbers of teachers, lack of books and other materials. Many of the new telecommunications technologies such as television, video and computer-based programmes may not be in use in Kenya yet, but in the meantime, the printed word is highly valued by students. In rural areas where there are few libraries, newspapers and books, anything in print is greatly sought after and avidly read by many people. As a result, distance education courses, even if based mainly on printed materials, fill a great need. They reach not only the target group but often find their way into the hands of numerous incidental learners. In this way, distance methods make the best use of what is available. They maximize the use of limited resources and extend education beyond classrooms and lecture halls at reasonably low cost.

What is needed now are ideas on how the new telecommunications technologies being used elsewhere in the world can be adapted for use in developing countries cheaply and in such numbers that all could benefit from them. When this happens and technology is used with the best teachers and back-up systems, there is no doubt that even greater strides will be made in distance education programmes and some of the present restraints will be overcome.

# Reference

Matiru, I.B. and Kamau, J. (1985) 'The Challenge of Distance Education for Inservice Teachers in Kenya: A Study to Assess the Effectiveness of the Distance Education Component of the Inservice Course for Untrained Primary School Teachers with Reference to the 1983-1985 Intake', *Proceedings of the Thirteenth World Conference, ICDE*, Melbourne, Australia, Paper 1014, August

**I. Barbara Matiru**, BA, MA *Br. Col.*

Senior Editor
Oxford University Press
Nairobi

Lecturer (part-time)
College of Adult and Distance Education
University of Nairobi
Kenya

Chapter Five

TOWARDS OPEN LEARNING

Jack Foks

## What is Open Learning?

The precise meaning of the term **open learning** is much debated in educational circles. While the debate may not have produced what purists would accept as a definition (for a discussion see Northcott, 1986), it has helped to determine certain things which open learning is not and to establish a list of open learning characteristics.

### What Open Learning is Not

First let us examine what open learning **is not.** It is not synonomous with electronically based communication technologies or, for that matter, other media such as human beings, printed materials, whiteboards and audio-visual resources. Certainly these have an important part to play in open learning, but they are simply a means of pursuing identified educational goals, not ends in themselves.

Open learning is not synonomous with distance education; nor is distance education a sub-set of open learning. Distance education is a mode of learning with certain characteristics which distinguish it from the campus-based mode of learning. It has been defined in various ways, and there is often a tendency to develop definitions which encompass desirable as well as necessary features. For example, in Australia, the Victorian Technical and Further Education Off-Campus Network (1985) has produced a list which contains both:

(1) Independent study, which, as far as is appropriate, provides students with the means to progress through sets of structured learning experiences at their own pace, at times and places of their own choosing.

(2) Self-instructional study materials which, as far as possible, are based on media and technologies most appropriate to the teaching/learning objectives and to the students' situations.

(3) One-to-one interaction between students and teachers operating at a distance.

The extent to which these characteristics incorporate phrases such as 'as far as appropriate' and 'as far as possible' should be noted. This could be seen as a realistic acceptance of the limitations on these characteristics which are imposed by:

(1) The knowledge, skills and attitudes of students and educators.

(2) The curricula and syllabuses of institutions.

(3) The accreditation and licensing requirements of courses.

(4) Community and industry attitudes towards education.

(5) The resources which are available to those responsible for the design, development, production and presentation of courses.

(6) The resources which are available to students.

Alternatively, it could be used as a self-protecting device by institutions which are more concerned with their own convenience than with serving their students. Institutions might accept distance education characteristics in principle but find that circumstances were such that unfortunately it was necessary to require distance education students to submit assignments according to a rigid schedule; to follow a predetermined sequence of instruction; to use one prescribed medium; to attend compulsory seminars or summer schools; and to sit for examinations at set times and places.

As a result, there would be only two of the distance education characteristics listed above which are necessary:

(1) The design, production and delivery of structured, self-instructional study materials.

(2) Regular one-to-one interaction between students and teachers operating at a distance from one another.

The other characteristics would be desirable ones to be achieved where possible. So, with sufficient will, ingenuity and capacity for self-justification, the distance education mode can be very closed indeed.

**The Characteristics of Open Learning**

What, then, are the characteristics of open learning?

Open learning is a state of mind. It is an approach taken to the planning, design, preparation and presentation of courses by educators, and an approach taken to the selection and use of learning strategies and associated resources by students. This approach seeks to provide students with as much choice and control as possible over content and learning strategies.

In an open learning approach, therefore, a number of factors must be taken into account. These factors are discussed below.

**The Size and Content of Open Learning Modules.** To allow maximum choice, the basic unit of learning should be as small as possible without undermining the educational integrity or logic of its content. Usually this will be a module based on a particular theme or topic - the basic unit or assignment of a distance education subject tends to correspond to this. Only rarely will it be a complete subject, and never a complete course. Such modules can then be combined in a variety of ways, or stand alone, to meet the various needs of students.

The content of the modules should be based on identified educational objectives which seek to meet the needs of students - this could require consultation, not only with industry, the community and fellow educators, but also with actual or potential students.

**Learning Strategies.** Educators must enable a range of learning strategies, each of which will achieve stated educational objectives, so that students have the opportunity to select the ones which best suit them. An important dimension along which strategies differ is the degree and nature of student/teacher interaction. On a continuum which ranges from no interaction to total interaction, three main types can be identified:

(1) Teacher-independent learning occurs when students learn without interaction with teachers, for example, working through a series of assignments or practical exercises at home, at work, or in the library.

(2) Delayed student/teacher interaction occurs when there are messages between students and teachers, but they are not delivered and received simultaneously. In other words, they are delayed due to the means of transmission, for example, the mail service, audio and video recordings, and so on. Delayed student/teacher interaction may be one-way or two-way.

(3) Immediate teacher/student interaction occurs when the messages between students and teachers are delivered and received at the same time, or virtually at the same time. This does not mean that they are necessarily involved in a face-to-face situation (although this could certainly be the case). They could be communicating by means of the telephone, electronic mail, facsimile, or semaphore.

**Learning Resources.** For any learning strategies to be used, a choice of resources has to made. Resources may be categorized into four main types:

(1) Human. This type of resource includes lecturers and tutors in the campus-based situation and it includes the markers of distance education assignments. It also includes other students and educators who act as referral agents and advisers.

(2) Print. There are two main types of print-based resources. The study guide is designed to lead students along a structured learning path. Textbooks and references provide information, some or all of which is useful to students, but they tend to be structured according to the authors' analyses of their subject matter, rather than the learning requirements of particular students.

(3) Audio-visual and electronic media. This category can be further divided according to the type of technology being considered - films, computers, television, audio recordings, overhead projectors and chalk, to name but a few. But there are also two other distinctions which can be made. The first is between one-way media, such as television broadcasts, and two-way media, such as telephones. The second is that these resources may be structured according to students' learning needs, for example, computer-aided instruction and notes on an overhead projector; or they may not be structured according to students' learning needs, for example, a current affairs programme broadcast on the radio.

(4) Facilities and equipment. This type of resource includes the facilities and equipment about which students must learn, and, as appropriate, which students must learn to use.

Educators need to consider, for each of the learning modules which they are planning, designing, preparing and presenting, the appropriate content, the range of available strategies and the range of available resources.

## Open Learning and Traditional Distinctions Between Modes

Open learning challenges distinctions which are commonly made between the campus-based and the distance education modes.

If one is concerned to provide students with meaningful choices, it is not useful to categorize various learning strategies as belonging solely to either mode. Even without the identification of open learning as such, there is much already occurring in education at all levels which tends to blur the edges of neat modal compartments. This blurring of the boundaries is reflected in three main types of activity:

(1) The inclusion, within a course of study formally identified as being based on one mode, of activities which would conform to the characteristics of the other mode. For example, a distance education course which includes summer schools, tutorials or seminars is making use of the face-to-face method. The classroom teacher who sends students out into the field on a research project which is to be written up at home, is using distance education methods.

(2) The emergence of learning strategies to which both campus-based and distance educators would lay claim. Examples include the use of computer-aided instruction to be performed in the library, self-paced activities in a workshop, and telephone tutorials.

(3) The use, by the exponents of one mode, of the resources developed for application in the other mode. Many distance educators complain bitterly about the devious means by which their campus-based

counterparts obtain distance education materials for use in face-to-face teaching. Alternatively, they exploit the demand for their materials by selling them. Similarly, there are occasions when distance educators use lecture notes or classroom resources as the basis for their teaching.

Open learning therefore is not about the mode of learning which is used. It is not about the needs of educators or institutions. It is about a student-oriented approach which designs programmes according to students' needs, which offers students as much choice as possible, and which sees learning methods and resources as means to educational goals.

If an open learning approach is taken, it is not useful to view the world of education in terms of sharply distinguished modes. Instead, educators should enable as wide a range of learning strategies as possible and develop a range of resources for learning, and not concern themselves with categories into which the methods and resources do or do not fit.

## The Students' Choices

Given that, in an open learning environment, there is a range of learning modules available, and that each of these has a range of methods and resources associated with it, students must choose the particular combinations of content, strategies and resources most likely to meet their needs.

But who determines what the needs of students are, and how these might best be met? A simplistic interpretation of open learning might lead to the answer that it is the student, and the student alone, who decides this. But how does this cater for the student who is uncertain or, even worse, mistaken? Student choice and control, which are so fundamental to open learning, can be seriously counter-productive if not combined with excellent counselling and the concept of student responsibility.

## Open Learning in the Technical and Further Education Sector

In the remainder of this Chapter, I will use the Technical and Further Education (TAFE) sector in Victoria, Australia as an example of a co-ordinated approach to open learning which is being introduced into a state-wide educational system.

### The Organization of TAFE

Victoria is a state in the south-east of Australia. It is the size of England and has a population of about four million. TAFE is an acronym for Technical and Further Education. In the past there was some debate about how it should be pronounced, but an academic of considerable repute resolved that it should rhyme with 'safe'. The TAFE sector of Australia's public education system provides post-compulsory education programmes which range from pre-apprentice to para-professional, and which cover vocational, access and continuing education. (See the ACOTAFE, 1974, report on needs in Technical and Further Education in Australia.)

The TAFE Board is the Victorian government body responsible for the co-ordination of TAFE in Victoria. Each of the Australian states and territories has its own TAFE co-ordinating authority, and the national government also has a body responsible for providing guidelines and special funding for TAFE across Australia.

Within TAFE in Victoria, there are the TAFE Board, eleven regional branches of the TAFE Board, and a variety of local TAFE providers, the largest of which are some thirty-two TAFE colleges. The other providers include a large and influential adult education organization; a significant multi-campus and multi-sector agricultural college; and a large number of small, local community providers.

In addition, there is an organization responsible for the development and delivery of distance education studies. It is called the Victorian TAFE Off-Campus Network and it consists of a central co-ordinating authority and eighteen member colleges, each of which has an 'off-campus centre' which is dedicated to providing general academic, pastoral and administrative support for the students who enrol through the Victorian TAFE Off-Campus Network. The Network's co-ordinating authority is known as the TAFE Off-Campus Co-ordinating Authority (TOCCA). It is the body which is responsible for co-ordinating the Open Learning Program which was introduced in 1986.

TAFE's Open Learning Program is significant for three reasons. The first is that it identifies open learning as a concept. The second is that it encourages the continuation of existing, and the introduction of new, open learning activities within TAFE's overall programme. The third is that it commits TAFE in Victoria to a co-ordinated approach to open learning.

### Issues in Implementing Open Learning in TAFE

An open learning programme will not succeed if the only persons attempting to put it into practice are the students and the designers of educational materials. Their efforts must be complemented by attitudinal, procedural and structural changes throughout the educational system. Amongst other things, open learning must be supported by appropriate and effective accreditation and approval procedures, counselling, ongoing learning management, and administrative systems. Given that there will be a variety of programmes selected by students who will then be working at different paces, times and places, the various support systems will need to be more sophisticated and flexible than those to which educators and administrators have become accustomed and committed. Such change need not involve leaping immediately behind the barricades; it will obviously be a gradual process, involving a considerable winning of hearts and minds. Nor need it aim to be universal - many traditional approaches will need to continue for a variety of educational, practical, industrial and political reasons.

So, to put it mildly, the scene is complex at both a formal and informal level, and this will have implications for TAFE's Open Learning Program. The comments which follow deal with some of the factors which will need to be considered in order to accommodate an open learning programme.

**Accreditation and Similar Games.** The majority of TAFE's offerings are long, formally accredited courses, often leading to qualifications or licences which entitle graduates to practise particular vocations. There is considerable input to the curricula and accreditation of such courses by unions, employers and government, and in a significant number of instances, accreditation is the responsibility of bodies outside TAFE. Within TAFE, the accreditation and approval procedures are part of a bureaucratic process which has not seriously taken into account the implications of open learning.

**Student Administration.** Enrolment procedures and the collection of student statistics are based upon certain assumptions which may impede the effective implementation of open learning. Two of these are a strictly defined academic year and the identification of a course as the basic enrolment unit. Both are criteria by which TAFE students must be identified if they are to be permitted to enrol. The ingenuity of counsellors, administrators and students is tested considerably when students wish to enrol in a mix of modules, from a variety of courses at different times each year.

**Cross-Creditation.** This refers to giving credit for studies undertaken elsewhere, and for work and life experience. Generally speaking, there is a tendency to refuse credit in all but the most obvious cases. This is not an unusual attitude in Australian educational institutions which have expended a good deal of effort to establish entry standards. However, in some courses, TAFE has introduced challenge exams and this goes some way towards alleviating problems associated with granting credit (see Foks 1982). Challenge exams provide the opportunity to obtain exemptions from those parts of a course in which students consider themselves to be proficient at the outset.

**Teaching Terms and Conditions.** Most TAFE teachers are

83

employed through a state-wide teaching service. Their terms and conditions are negotiated between the Victorian government and the major teachers' union. Open learning will affect such terms and conditions.

It will be necessary for teachers to act more as facilitators and less as omniscient lecturers, more as course designers and less as the sole learning resource. Not only will this involve possible changes to terms and conditions, but it challenges some of the measurements upon which those terms and conditions are based. How does one, for example, translate classroom teaching hours into the time taken to design learning materials or to manage students' learning?

**Co-ordination or Control.** There are many resources already available in TAFE which have the potential to contribute to open learning. Providers often have talent, expertise and facilities available which have been accumulated over time and which have been used in a variety of ways. Indeed, there are already examples of open learning in TAFE, even though they have not necessarily been identified as such, and even though they have not been part of a co-ordinated approach.

It could easily happen that TOCCA begins to build up its own central pool of resources and expertise with a view to developing everything centrally. This would be an exercise in expensive duplication and might alienate local TAFE personnel. The TAFE policy on open learning therefore makes specific reference to exploiting the potential of existing expertise and resources in order to achieve cost-effectiveness and a sense of involvement by all the players in TAFE.

The other inclination of central co-ordinating authorities is to develop drawn-out and complex bureaucratic procedures. These are usually justified in terms of a need for accountability when large amounts of public funds are to be committed. Certainly, accountability is important, but the assumption often is that it needs to be before the event, and that this can only be guaranteed by the provision of detailed plans and budgets, based on extensive research. If TOCCA is to facilitate speedy and flexible responses, then it must be prepared to

84

support concept proposals at short notice, with the proviso that accountability will be in the form of reports and evaluations prepared during and after the implementation of projects.

**Open Learning and Distance Education Students.** Open learning should provide new and exciting choices for all students. However, it could easily happen that these choices are only made available to students who are already well looked after, and that, in the process, one loses sight of those students for whom distance education opportunities were first established. There is therefore a risk that TOCCA will become so absorbed in the glamour and/or frustrations of getting open learning going, that it will forget its original clients.

This should not happen if open learning is properly implemented, that is, if students and their needs are clearly identified and learning programmes are designed and implemented accordingly. Nevertheless, two safeguards will be necessary, just to make sure.

First, open learning programmes should be designed with distance education students identified as the primary targets. Programmes which are developed on this basis will certainly still be useful for other students, whereas the converse is not usually true.

Second, the special support systems which have been developed for distance education students, such as counselling, the handling and monitoring of assignments, and specialized learning management, should continue to be made available.

## Government Policy and Open Learning

An open learning approach provides a significant means of implementing government policies on social justice and access to education; economic rationalization and manpower planning; and sharing of resources.

At the time of writing, there is in office a Victorian government which is committed to a number of pro-active policies, and which sees the TAFE system very much as an arm of government which will implement appropriate parts of those policies. Open learning is seen as one means by which TAFE can do this.

**Social Justice and Access.** The Victorian government's social justice policy seeks to overcome disadvantage within the community and has two broad implications for education. It means that members of the community must be helped to overcome educational disadvantage and that education must be used to help them overcome social and/or vocational disadvantage.

One of the prime objectives of open learning is to gear learning to the needs of students. If those students are persons for whom traditional learning methods are inappropriate, then alternative methods will need to be provided. Adults with social and work commitments, geographically isolated persons, house-bound women, physically or mentally disabled persons, aborigines and the young unemployed are some groups for whom regular attendance at TAFE colleges at set times may well not be appropriate, and these are certainly among the groups identified by government as requiring special assistance to overcome educational disadvantage.

If they are to overcome social or vocational disadvantage, some of these persons may require basic training, some may require re-training, some may require remediation or bridging studies, some may require long, formal courses, and others may require short, special purpose courses. Although the stated outcomes of, say, an introductory course in bookkeeping, may be the same for each of these groups in terms of the concepts, skills and knowledge which are to be developed, the logic, structure and pace of the programme will almost certainly need to be different in each case.

In the past, these persons have often been required to enrol in those existing programmes which come closest to meeting their needs. An open learning approach is required to guarantee that the content, structure and duration of offerings are wholly appropriate.

Overcoming the impediments to access to TAFE courses was one of the reasons why the Victorian TAFE Off-Campus Network was established in the first place. In Victoria, as elsewhere, distance education was seen as a means of increasing access, and the introduction of open learning, on a co-ordinated state-wide basis, is taking the notion of access several steps further.

**Economic Policies.** Both at the state and national levels, governments look to TAFE to contribute to their economic and labour market policies. As well as developing its own economic policy for the 1980s (see Victorian State Government, 1984), the Victorian government has responded to policies developed by the Australian federal government. The open learning approach is seen to assist the implementation of these policies in three ways.

First, in common with other publicly funded educational systems around the world, TAFE is being asked to do more for less. Because of the emphasis on co-ordination combined with the use of existing resources, its open learning programme seeks to avoid wasteful duplication or the allocation of resources to develop learning programmes which are educationally ineffective. In addition to the cost efficiencies that a co-ordinated approach should bring, there are further efficiencies inherent in the nature of an open learning approach which is not dependent upon:

(1) The use of capital intensive buildings. Students do not necessarily have to attend campus-based classes.

(2) The provision of expensive and quickly out-dated facilities. For example, the use of new technologies to provide simulated exercises, or project work conducted on the job, can help to reduce the need for high capital investment.

(3) Having to cover the cost of travel and accommodation necessary for students to attend campus-based classes.

It may come as no surprise that these are advantages also associated with the distance education mode.

Second, both state and federal governments are concerned with Australia's internal and international trading situation. The packages developed as part of open learning programmes are considered to be marketable commodities both to sections of industry and the community, and to an education-hungry third world.

Finally, and perhaps most importantly, open learning is expected to be a significant way of providing flexible and relevant training to support the state and federal governments' manpower planning programmes, which range from training unemployed youth so that they may acquire the skills necessary to enter and stay in the workforce, through to retraining adults, already in the workforce, whose skills have become out-dated.

The expectations of open learning in TAFE are very much based on the United Kingdom's Open Tech programme (see Ashurst, 1986 and Gould, 1986), which was set up to help deal with a situation much like Australia's, namely a dramatic shift from an industrial to an information-based society, and an increasingly competitive world market in raw materials, manufactured goods and information technologies. As a result of these trends, the United Kingdom had a workforce and a large number of unemployed people whose skills required continuous and speedy modification. The Open Tech's emphasis on student needs, flexibility, entrepreneurial relationships with industry and ultimate financial self-reliance, was intended to deal with this.

The establishment of the Open Tech reflected a government view that traditional education and training systems could not cope with these new demands. This attitude was reflected further in the Open Tech's approach to projects. Public education had to compete with private educational organizations and with industry to obtain funds for projects which were expected to be self-funding within three years. In Australia there is also a growing awareness in the public education and training sectors that the slow response times and self-centred approaches of the past are no longer appropriate, and that the community, government and industry will look elsewhere if changes are not made - there are already indications that, in Australia as in North America, industry is organizing its own training because it is frustrated at public education's lack of responsiveness.

The Open Tech is therefore considered to provide something of a model for open learning in TAFE. It also provides a dilemma for those who consider that TAFE should not be narrowly vocational and should be publicly funded: Open Tech is based on the 'user pays' principle.

**Sharing of Resources.** There is considerable encouragement by the Victorian government for all types of co-operation in education. This is due to a number of factors. At its most practical, it is a response to more difficult economic times with a corresponding need for sharing wherever possible; at a more altruistic level, it seeks to provide the most educationally effective and appropriate learning to those who need it.

Open learning generally can be part of such co-operation. But there is a particular aspect of open learning which makes co-operation relevant and possible, namely the learning resources developed to support its programmes. This is especially true of resources based on the new electronic technologies, which require considerable sophistication and development, and whose delivery mechanisms allow wide transmission.

As far as TAFE is concerned, the sharing of resources and involvement in co-operative ventures can take place within the system, that is, among providers and between the bodies responsible for the distance education and the campus-based modes. The blurring of distinctions between modes of learning, government pressure and market forces all encourage such co-operation.

In addition TAFE in Victoria will need to involve itself in a variety of working relationships with:

(1) TAFE in other states. This already takes place to an extent, especially in the form of nationally developed curricula and the sharing of distance education materials.

(2) Other sectors of education. This, of course, raises questions regarding standards, accreditation and the granting of credit, but there are already some interesting examples of co-operation such as the use of Sunraysia College of TAFE's facilities and staff for the delivery of parts of the Ballarat College of Advanced Education's programme, and the Victorian TAFE Off-Campus Network acting as an agent of the Darling Downs Institute of Advanced Education in the provision of continuing education courses. Government and economic pressures will, as they have in the United Kingdom and North America, lead to more co-operation.

(3) Other sections of government. As is the case elsewhere, there are a number of government departments and authorities interested in education and, in particular, training. These include departments of labour, health, social services, science and technology, communications, finance and foreign affairs.

(4) Industry. Once again, the Open Tech sets an example which is consistent with TAFE's charter to respond to industry's needs. Governments are now encouraging a range of forms of co-operation, including joint developments, industry sponsorship, and on-the-job training facilities and activities.

In conclusion, open learning seeks to provide students with as much control and choice as possible of the content, time, place, pace and method of their learning. Open learning should not be equated with any one mode of learning, nor should its learning resources automatically be based on any one medium or technology. Instead, various approaches and media, or combinations of approaches and media, should be used according to the needs of students and the educational objectives of programmes.

TAFE in Victoria is introducing open learning as part of its overall programme. By doing so within a co-ordinated framework, it seeks to exploit, in an educationally effective and cost-effective way, the very real potential that open learning has to contribute to government policies on social justice, economic development and manpower planning.

But TAFE will need to proceed with some care. There are many entrenched attitudes, systems and procedures which will need to be changed without losing the good will of those who may be affected. And it will be necessary to ensure that traditional distance education students are not forgotten as more and more opportunities are provided to their more privileged campus-based counterparts. Open learning should therefore be introduced gradually, initially concentrating on those areas most receptive to its underlying philosophy; and it should take into account the special needs of distance education students as it designs, develops and presents its learning programmes and associated learning resources.

# References

ACOTAFE (1974) *TAFE in Australia - Report on Needs in Technical and Further Education*, Commonwealth of Australia

Ashurst, J.G. (1986) 'Open Learning in the Open Tech Program in the U.K.: Lessons for TAFE in Victoria', *Victorian TAFE Papers Number 5*, TAFE Educational Services Co-ordinators' Association and Hawthorn Institute of Education

Foks, J. (1982) *A Report on a Study Tour of the USA and Canada*, Royal Melbourne Institute of Technology, Melbourne

Gould, L.A. (1986) *Open Learning - An Education and Training Programme for TAFE Victoria*, Victorian TAFE Board, 20 February

Northcott, P. (1986) 'Distance Education and Open Education: An Exploration of the Terms', *Open Campus*, **12**, Deakin University, Geelong, pp. 34-40

Victorian State Government (1984) *Victoria. The Next Step. Economic Initiatives and Opportunities for the 1980s,* Government of Victoria, 9 April

Victorian Technical and Further Education Off-Campus Network (1985) *TAFE Off-Campus Information '85,* Royal Melbourne Institute of Technology, Melbourne, p. 1

**Jack G.H. Foks**, BA *Melb.,* TSTC *Hawthorn*

Head
Victorian TAFE Off-Campus Network
Australia

Chapter Six

# COLLABORATION BETWEEN THE INDUSTRIAL AND EDUCATIONAL SECTORS

Tom Ledwidge and Frank Miller

Those who are responsible for industry in Australia are required to manage organizations which are subject to rapid and accelerating technological change. This, in turn, places a heavy demand on members of the workforce to engage in education and training if they are to maintain a high level of technological competence.

Universities and colleges are likewise under pressure to deal with technological change. This affects their curricula, academic and administrative staff, and students.

Although industry and academia are both faced with common educational and training problems arising from the rapid spread of technology, the educational goals of these two sectors are often quite divergent.

While institutions of higher education may graduate only a proportion of the students who enrol in them, employers in industry need to achieve much higher success rates: they cannot afford to waste the effort involved in training their staff or to employ a workforce which is only partially competent. Employers are often unable to survive economically if their staff perform at lower than mastery (that is, full competence) level.

If levels of competence decline the result might be the demise of industrial society as we know it. Indeed, according to the Organization for Economic Co-operation and Development, the process of decline appears to have begun already, causing Australia to slide down the pole in the competitive world scene.

93

Economic theory suggests that if indexed wage payments are not balanced by increasing productivity then an unstable situation will result and security of employment will be jeopardized. This form of instability is increasing in Australia, especially in occupations which are directly funded by governments and which traditionally have been associated with job security. Inevitably those organizations which are unable to increase the productivity of their workforces at a rapid rate, at a time when operational costs are also increasing, may be forced to reduce the numbers that they employ. Can this situation be reversed? Can staff competence levels be maintained so that employees provide value for money to employers on a continuing basis despite the effects of technological change? What is the relevance of the educational sector in this process?

In this Chapter we argue that the time has arrived when the issues of access to education and training, and the levels of competence achieved, must be addressed by both the industrial and educational sectors in a co-ordinated way.

Our argument is based on the premise that the current divergence of the aims of higher education and industry must be halted. We are particularly concerned about the disparity which exists between the realities of the world of work and the outcomes of the formal educational process.

For instance, the role of compulsory schooling, although changing, continues to be largely one of teaching subjects which are relevant, not for transition to work, but to enable a small percentage of students to achieve university entrance. Those who do not qualify, emerge from their school years ill-equipped to meet the requirements of the workplace.

Initial qualifications, which are obtained prior to employment, simply cannot afford to be inappropriate to the realities of the world of work. Furthermore, continuing education and training are essential if members of the workforce are to maintain their effectiveness. If we accept that education is a lifelong process, extending well beyond initial qualifications, and that the environment of most individuals will be dominated by employment in some form for a large part of life, then an acceptable strategy for promoting lifelong

94

learning would include a substantial degree of co-operation between the industrial and educational sectors. Later in this Chapter, some of the forms of collaboration which could promote closer co-operation between the aims and activities of these two sectors are presented.

## Issues in Training the Workforce

### Collaboration Between Sectors

Collaboration between industry and higher education in the development of industry-specific training programmes, although well established in other countries, is not a common phenomenon in Australia. This is unfortunate for many reasons, not the least of which is the opportunity collaboration provides to earn knowledge-derived export income.

We realize that for many academics in universities the idea of co-operation with industry is an anathema. To adopt such a stance in the context of a college of advanced education, however, denies the brief of these institutions to provide vocational education which serves the needs of the community and, in particular, to prepare professional and para-professional workers for industry, commerce and the public service. Over the years, as a result of public demand, considerable diversity has developed in the range and type of courses now offered by the colleges. The inclusion of courses in arts and education, for example, has meant that the emphasis on the technologies and applied sciences is less pronounced in colleges of advanced education than was originally envisaged.

Although universities are distinguished by their research activities their role is not totally divorced from industry. Though the time available for academics to collaborate with industry is limited, departments such as engineering usually undertake some consulting and contract work in industry and their specialization and expertise can be a valuable aid.

Some successful joint-venture training programmes have been undertaken in Queensland between the Queensland

Electricity Commission and both Darling Downs Institute of Advanced Education and Queensland Institute of Technology. The project undertaken with Darling Downs Institute of Advanced Education is concerned with development of self-paced learning programmes for transmission staff who need to update their skills in microprocessor technology. This project is scheduled for completion in 1987. The project undertaken with Queensland Institute of Technology (see Chesmond, Cook and Miller, 1986) was concerned with instrumentation and control technology for power station technicians. This was completed successfully in 1985.

Although many joint-venture initiatives have been undertaken world-wide (see Beder, 1984), not all have been successful. As usual, the failures are more informative than the successes. The failures of inter-organizational collaboration can be attributed to lack of candour in communication; poor selection of partners (resulting in operational incompatibility); inadequacies in initial planning and in contract negotiation; failure to implement programmes as mutually intended; and failure to evaluate the potential benefits and possible disadvantages to both parties early enough.

Where joint-venture training programme development is undertaken by educational institutions at industry's initiative, funding for such activity should be provided by industry. Contractual agreements are required to protect the interests of both parties and these need to explore and resolve such issues as:

(1) The structure of learning packages.

(2) The ancillary learning resources required.

(3) The ownership of copyright.

(4) The distribution of royalties.

96

(5) Photocopying rights.

(6) Marketing rights.

(7) The freedom to modify material.

(8) The package production rate.

In all, the message is clear: without pre-planning, openness, trust, commitment and structure, collaborative ventures between education and industry are not guaranteed to succeed.

## Appraising the Needs of Learners

Initial education and continuing education and training need to be founded on an appraisal of what it is that learners actually need to know and what skills they need to master in order to achieve higher levels of competence.

Many students who are taking an initial qualification seek to make an early commitment to a specific career objective. It is the educator's responsibility to help them make their goals viable, by guiding their study and helping them develop those qualities which are judged to be necessary in achieving this.

On the other hand, some students enter colleges and universities with an open mind as to their ultimate career goal. In this case, it is the educator's responsibility to recognize that career decisions may be more easily taken by students who have some knowledge outside their own tentative field of specialization, together with some understanding of the relationship between technology and society.

The fraction of first-level students who would wish to exercise some degree of choice has not been the subject of any serious study to date. It may, however, be significant. For example, in a recent sample of over a thousand students in the United Kingdom enrolled in science and technology courses, approximately half of first-year science students and a third of first-year technology students had a completely open mind as to which career path they wished to follow.

It would appear, therefore, that educators should ensure that students entering courses are presented with a curriculum which embodies a flexibility of career choices. This need not preclude the provision of syllabus choices to cater for narrower career paths for those who seek them. Students, for the most part, seek involvement, relevance and stimulation in the courses offered to them. Their needs are complex and challenging.

In continuing education, industry is a major part of the learning environment: hence it plays an essential role in the lifelong learning process. The work situation needs careful integration into the total programme of instruction if it is to contribute to it in a meaningful way.

A course of study, therefore, is not a description of how training time will be spent, but a definition of what students will know and/or be able to do at the end of the programme. It is in the identification of these learning outcomes that industrial representatives have a key role to perform. Objectives like 'para-professional education will increasingly be required to produce graduates with a down-to-earth middle perspective' need to be operationalized to enable learning activities to be designed. It then becomes the educator's job to design a curriculum to achieve the learning objectives. Educators should also build in objectives to make the students aware of a broader perspective.

Frequent communication between the industrial and educational sectors is needed if joint-venture programme development is to be successful. This will focus on specification of objectives, the design of curricula, and the development of appropriate instructional methods.

Two examples of such joint-venture curriculum appraisals in which the authors participated are those of investigations in the Queensland Electricity Commission and in the Brisbane Boys' College, a private secondary school.

In 1986, an investigation was completed within the Queensland Electricity Commission which looked at the needs for technical competency of a selection of mature-aged power station control systems technicians working in an environment of rapidly changing technology. The study set out to identify

98

those training-related issues which employers need to understand if they are to manage their workforces in an efficient and cost effective way. A major feature of the investigation was the recognition at the outset that 'learning' was in fact a more important issue than 'teaching': whilst learning may well result from teaching, teaching itself cannot guarantee learning. The research team were particularly concerned to assist employees whose formal education was completed several years before but whose learning fears persisted: a legacy of their often unsatisfactory schooling experiences. In fact, the reaction of some of the organization's potential adult learners to the prospect of classroom learning and of exam competition was severe. It was clear that learning would have to be made palatable if it were to be successful. Individualization and substantial tutorial support would be required virtually on demand. It was anticipated that this latter requirement was going to be difficult to achieve, since tutors would have to be drawn from technical supervisors whose work responsibilities would preclude easy availability.

The problem of on-demand support was resolved by Queensland Electricity Commission through modularization of learning material (made available in the form of printed booklets for use in a stand-alone self-paced mode) and the use of computer terminals (one terminal per power station) to provide formative testing on demand to trainees and which would also generate status reports for supervisor/tutors so that they could be kept aware daily of the learning progress of their staff. It was decided that the computer support system should not have an instructional function, since it was considered that it would generally not be cost-justifiable to translate learning material into the machine at that stage.

This pragmatic approach, a result of the combined engineering/educational backgrounds of the project team, resulted in considerable cost savings in hardware and time spent in instructional design while continuing to support personal and individualized learning styles.

In addition, this study identified a number of goals which would have to be achieved if proposals for further training expenditure were to be taken seriously. Such proposals need to:

(1) Provide for effective cost-control of training.

(2) Significantly improve access to economic training.

(3) Reduce the training administration burden.

(4) Improve training cost-effectiveness.

(5) Alleviate learning fears in mature-age employees.

(6) Respond to individual learning needs.

(7) Monitor and ensure learning outcomes.

It was clear that any serious attempt to improve learning achievement must recognize employees' individual learning rates and styles; motivation; previous experience; availability of time to study in the light of work commitments; the extent of knowledge and skills required; and the necessity for employees to achieve mastery.

A research project based upon similar administrative problems and learning needs was undertaken at Brisbane Boys' College in connection with a grade nine computer studies course.

The success in terms of learner satisfaction achieved in both these projects suggests that adult learning principles can be productively applied even at school level. (See Miller, 1986 and Miller and Cook, 1986 for a more detailed account of these projects.) This finding is encouraging, particularly in the face of mounting evidence that the relationship between teaching and learning is not clear and that teacher effects on learner achievement are unstable, with much teaching behaviour being unrelated to learning outcomes.

We believe that by adopting an approach which emphasizes learning as distinct from teaching, both employers and employees would benefit in ways that do not stem from teacher-centred approaches to education.

## Devising Appropriate Training Programmes

Provision of training programmes for employees is a major problem facing many organizations, especially when they operate from a number of locations over a substantial geographical area. The problem is compounded when an organization is involved in a wide range of activities and where at a given time there may be only small numbers of staff requiring training in specific areas of competency.

Traditional educational approaches are frequently unable to provide access to the kind of training which is necessary for industry or to guarantee the cost-effectiveness of the investment made in training by industry. Where the educational sector cannot provide appropriate types and levels of training, industries are forced to emphasize inservice education and training.

There are usually significant problems associated with attendance by employees at short courses provided by manufacturers, equipment suppliers, universities, colleges of advanced education and technical colleges. Of necessity these organizations must target programmes for a relatively broad cross-section of employers. Some specific problems are:

(1) The high cost of registration, travel and accommodation, usually restrict the number of employees who can attend.

(2) Inappropriate timing and frequency of courses.

(3) Limited availability of places on courses.

(4) Operating constraints which prevent the release of more than a few employees at a time.

(5) Limited relevance of the syllabuses (often discovered too late).

(6) Courses normally aimed at a broad target population are rarely satisfactory in terms of the breadth, depth and pace of delivery.

(7) The limited adequacy of course handouts.

(8) Inadequate sensitivity to learning styles, capacities and experience of participants.

(9) The difficulty of evaluating the extent and effectiveness of the learning achieved.

(10) The unlikelihood that participants will pass on their newly acquired knowledge effectively to other employees.

Many of the problems identified above apply equally in the case of short courses in industry provided by permanent or guest trainers, and as a result the cost-effectiveness of formal classroom-based programmes is being increasingly challenged.

Rather than adjusting to the rigid scheduling of educational institutions at a time when the need for staffing constraints requires increased productivity from all employees, alternative solutions must be sought by industry.

Evidence points to the fact that distance education is as effective as campus-based education for motivated and supported students and also suggests that distance education methods are as effective for employees under the age of twenty years as they are for older employees. The evidence that self-directed learning is an attractive and effective process is increasingly persuasive. Industry is fast coming to recognize the value of individualized learning approaches using modularized materials and of computer-based technology, all of which are increasingly identified with distance education.

Courses offered in the distance education mode are designed to be complete in themselves, and ideally should not rely on other inputs to ensure that the average student succeeds. It is, however, generally accepted that the provision of additional help will reduce the attrition rate and help students to achieve a higher grade than they would have done otherwise.

In the case of some courses in Engineering and Surveying offered by the Darling Downs Institute of Advanced Education in Queensland, the extra help to enhance the programme is provided by 'industrial tutors' who are appointed as honorary members of the Institute on the recommendation of their employer. In some cases the employer provides funds for the payment of tutors. One particularly successful example of the scheme is in the area of Civil Engineering where cadets of the Main Roads Department are enrolled as distance education students in an associate diploma course. By the very nature of the Main Roads Department's responsibilities, the cadets and their supervisors are sparsely distributed over the whole of Queensland with one or two engineers and two or three cadets forming a working unit; one of the engineers assumes the role of the industrial tutor and meets with the cadets on a regular basis. The industrial tutor becomes a role model, a mentor, and in many cases an academic tutor. Almost unconsciously, the industrial tutor also assumes a pastoral-care role and provides feedback advice to the course designers at each regular course review.

The scheme in its present form works well in situations similar to the Main Roads Department environment, but presents a challenge of a different nature when the industrial activity is concentrated at a number of geographical locations and where student numbers are significant in each location. The desire of a significant number of the engineers to assist is only too clearly evident and ways are currently under investigation by which this goodwill and talent can be co-ordinated and integrated into the total learning environment.

Many distance education programmes require that a period of time is spent on-campus at a residential school to undertake practical work. Residential schools are usually of one to two weeks' duration, sometimes occur more than once per year, and are usually during school holiday periods. This can be quite inconvenient for many employees, particularly those who are married with children, and whose only opportunity to take recreation leave occurs during such periods.

103

Faced with this problem, the Queensland Electricity Commission established a joint-venture arrangement in 1981 with Darling Downs Institute of Advanced Education whereby students could undertake residential school practical work at their place of work (in this case at Gladstone Power Station), under the supervision of a supervisor/tutor accredited for this purpose by the Institute. In this way, controlled work experience relevant to the subject being studied was able to be provided, making use of equipment with which the student was to some extent already familiar, and which was often more sophisticated and modern than that available on the campus.

Employer costs associated with the provision of relief staff to prevent disruption to work caused by the release of employees to attend residential schools are substantial and are increasingly being seen as unacceptable. The case for greater flexibility is obvious.

## Forms of Collaboration

In this section we present a number of ideas about forms of collaboration which could be used to promote closer co-operation between the industrial and educational sectors and to improve the effectiveness of education and training for the workforce in ways that would benefit both sectors.

### Project Sponsorship

Project sponsorship is an approach to collaboration which is not widely employed but which offers significant benefits both to employers and to educational institutions. Project sponsorships involve the provision of modest financial support by employers to projects of final-year students. (They are usually associated with engineering courses.) A number of benefits accrue from such an arrangement, for example:

(1) The quality of the project is enhanced considerably.

(2) Early communication between employers and the student's course supervisor in relation to the project increases the relevance of the project work to industry and relieves stress on academics who otherwise are required to create projects *in vacuo*.

(3) If the employer can provide an in-house supervisor in addition to the student's course supervisor, this person can liaise with the educational institution throughout the life of the project. Because sponsorships are given to projects which have industrial applications, such ongoing communication between an employer and an institution is very beneficial.

(4) Scope exists for extended support for projects in the form of temporary loans of equipment, trips to industrial sites, and access to a range of staff as well as to specific technical information.

(5) The prospects of future employment for project-sponsored students is enhanced.

Project sponsorships are, in effect, a cost-effective co-operative effort between the industrial and educational sectors, and they deserve to be used more widely.

**Teaching Company Schemes**

In Australia, the federal Department of Industry, Technology and Commerce administers a teaching company scheme - an idea derived from a scheme in the United Kingdom which has the potential to link industry and education in a most productive way. Basically the Government provides half the salary and overheads required for a commercial company to employ a top quality, experienced graduate. The company must work in partnership, on a defined project, with an educational institution, which receives a grant to cover administrative costs.

The Department of Industry, Technology and Commerce evaluates submissions and makes recommendations to the appropriate federal Minister on the establishment of suitable teaching companies.

The scheme aims to raise industrial performance through effective and long-term access to academic expertise and to the research facilities of educational institutions. It is hoped that the scheme will help Australian industry to plan and develop products that may be sold to overseas markets. In achieving these aims it is expected that a number of other benefits will accrue. For those academics who engage in a teaching company scheme, their research interests may be more attuned to the needs of industry and enhance the relevance of both their teaching and their research. The very existence of the scheme provides talented graduates with appropriate training for careers in industry. Overall the scheme is a very effective strategy for inducing collaboration between the industrial and educational sectors.

**Research Companies Based in Academia**

The idea of forming a commercial research company based within an institution of higher education is barely a quarter of a century old in Australia, having its origin in the formation of Uni-Search at the University of New South Wales. Initially the concept was regarded with some suspicion by academics, who thought that engaging in research which aimed to solve problems for industry was intellectually inferior to basic research.

It took considerable patience and leadership on the part of the foundation head of Uni-Search to coax the first few academics to use their research skills on problems based in industry. As it happened the first two years of Uni-Search saw the solution of several major problems, thus establishing the company on a firm foundation. Academics quickly came to realize that the source of the problem was largely irrelevant in determining its intellectual level and that the presence of a client who had deadlines to meet acted as a stimulus to the research. The financial rewards for academics were also set at an attractive level with many of those participating almost doubling their university salaries.

The Uni-Search company grew rapidly and within two years of its foundation, the head was transferred from a part-time appointment to a full-time one and the turnover reached tens of millions of dollars. By any measure it was a success and acted as a model for other institutions to follow. All Australian states now house research companies which act as commercial arms of higher education institutions. The latest addition is Uni-Quest at the University of Queensland, which followed on from the successful operation of Q-Search at the Queensland Institute of Technology.

In 1984, the Queensland Minister of Education established a working party to give advice on how the many technological innovations arising through Q-Search, Uni-Quest and from other educational sources in Queensland could be brought to the attention of the wider community. One of the major recommendations of the working party was for the establishment of an electronic data base which would contain up-to-date information about innovations which are occurring in Queensland's higher education institutions. The data base known as QTECH is now available world-wide and, together with the research companies, provides a stimulus for even greater collaboration between industry and education.

## Career Counselling

Career guidance is always in demand, especially in times of severe labour-market competition such as exists currently in the Australian economic climate.

Career counselling has always been the province of the educational sector, whether at the compulsory schooling level or at the higher education level. Much justifiable criticism has been levelled at such counselling, the major criticism being a failure to appreciate the employer's perspective.

Counselling is often viewed as a part-time activity, and it has failed to address school-to-work issues effectively: a consequence of an increasing demand to attend to more

107

pressing issues such as home-school liaison. This is notwithstanding the genuine and dedicated efforts of counsellors themselves. What is required is a credible and effective career guidance process which gains its strength by maintaining strong links with employer groups, educational institutions, employee organizations, professional associations and government departments and agencies.

Collaboration in this area will be enhanced by support from broadly-based associations of career guidance officers assisting the community to make initial and mid-life career decisions with confidence based upon the knowledge that the guidance information is thoroughly reliable in a broad and realistic context.

**Course Assessment and Design**

One of the most important areas in which industry can, and should, make a significant contribution to collaboration is in the design and assessment of courses taught in institutions of higher education. Regrettably many academics work almost in isolation when designing courses. As a result courses often lack relevance to industry. Sometimes an attempt to give validity to a new course proposal is made by including a token industry representative on a course design team which consists mainly of academics. Depending on the strength and vision of the representative such a strategy is likely to remain cosmetic only.

Happily the current trend, certainly in the higher education sector in Queensland, is to have a course assessment committee with a majority of its membership from the industrial sector. The inherent risk with such a committee, however, is that they may design a course which is highly relevant to industry, producing graduates with immediately useful skills but lacking the intellectual flexibility to grow and develop in the future. To avoid such an obvious pitfall the team must rely on the skill and leadership of the committee's chairman and the intrinsic professionalism of the committee members.

While the benefits of the forms of collaboration outlined above may seem obvious, the important issue concerns the

108

consequences of non-collaboration. If collaboration does not take place, employees in industry will find that it becomes harder and harder to maintain a high level of competence in the face of technological change. If competence is not maintained industry will be unable to keep pace in the competitive world scene.

## The Contribution of Continuing Education to Collaboration

Perhaps the most important factors influencing moves towards collaboration between industry and academia are the policies and codes of professional bodies in Australia; the examples set by professional bodies in other countries; and the attitudes of the people involved in the collaborative process. Formal continuing education is a vital element in each of these factors.

In the engineering profession, the value of continuing education, both in nature and scope, has been debated extensively, but until quite recently the outcomes of the debate were inconclusive. However, in 1986 the Institution of Engineers, Australia, adopted a policy that encourages professional engineers to undertake continuing education activities.

The Institution recognizes that, as a nation, we have developed a sound scientific base which is not significantly different from our competitors in the world marketplace, but that our engineering dimension needs to be developed.

Despite estimates that the 'half life' of a professional engineer is between four and ten years, the Institution chose not to make the activities mandatory. It argued that the code of ethics obliges professional engineers to maintain professional competence by updating knowledge and skills and that this in itself is sufficient, if employers and providers of education play their part. It remains to be seen if the appeal by the Institution to the code of ethics will have the desired effect.

Examples of continuing education for professionals are available to Australia. For instance in the United States such education accelerated rapidly in 1984 with the formation of the National Technological University which aimed to establish itself as the model for continuing education. In 1985 this University became the first satellite network to broadcast two channels of full motion video on one transponder. Thirty per cent of the programmes are broadcast live and interactively and are supplemented with electronic mail to enhance the students' ability to keep in touch with academics.

In 1986 the National Technological University comprised twenty-one participating universities and seventy-one industry-based sponsoring sites. Each university is the location of an up-link to a satellite. The National Technological University with the Association for Media-Based Continuing Education for Engineers can provide access for engineers at the seventy-one participating companies to nearly ninety per cent of all university produced, media-based, courses and seminars. As Garry (1986) pointed out, 'The National Technological University creates the mechanism by which the best technical and intellectual resources of American higher education can be made available to every corner of our country. ( ... ) The National Technological University will play an important role in increasing the international competitiveness of American industry.' (p.4).

The fact that so many organizations in the United States co-operate in the provision of lifelong education for the nation's engineers not only illustrates the positive benefits of collaboration but provides a model which we in Australia would be wise to consider, if only to adopt a co-operative posture within our own shores. The key to achieving continuing education for professionals would appear to be in the attitudes of employers, academics and clients. Stokes (1986) makes this point. 'Employers (in Australia) with very few exceptions have been reluctant to acknowledge the need for continuing education as a regular part of the professional development of their staff ( ... ) Many individual employees have been reluctant to bear part of the cost of continuing education as a reasonable contribution to their own development' (p.2).

Employer and employee attitudes need to change or be changed if the goal of at least maintaining our share of an international market is to be realized. If a relatively densely populated and rich nation like the United States finds it beneficial to focus on a national collaborative continuing education network, then perhaps Australia should do likewise.

In conclusion, the pace of technological change is forcing industry to invest larger and larger sums in the maintenance of staff competence, particularly in engineering and scientific areas. The attitude of educational institutions towards both initial and continuing education is changing rapidly towards one of partnership with industry in order to achieve what is increasingly being identified as a common goal - that of ensuring the continuing competence of all employees.

Information is spread so diffusely today, that institutions of higher education, which have been traditionally the repository of specialist knowledge, must re-examine the relevance of their role. It is unlikely that any professionals working in industry would seriously consider returning to a campus-based institution to update for technological change in the workplace. Firstly there would not be the time, and secondly formal institutions may be unable to assist.

Survival in the face of rapidly changing technology has now become a matter of adapting to new knowledge and of developing effective techniques of learning. Classroom-oriented methods are rapidly losing their relevance in this regard. Modern educators must recognize this and extend their professional competence into the field of learning effectiveness. They should also become experts in how and where to find knowledge and in the ways and means of best mastering knowledge at appropriate levels.

Industry, faced with the necessity of ensuring the continuing competence of staff in a rapidly changing work environment, can ill afford to overlook initiatives based on distance education and computer-based learning technology if its staff are to survive the increasing pressure to adapt to the changing demands made upon them.

Computer management of learning (CML) where learning materials remain external to the computer and where the computer is employed in prescribing and administering the learning process, but not as a vehicle for instruction, offers the potential for supporting the individual learning needs of each employee on a continuing cost-effective and non-competitive basis (see Miller, Cook and Clark, 1986). It offers what appears to be a realistic solution to the hitherto insoluble problem of maintaining employee competence irrespective of age, experience, learning rate, geographical location, years from formal schooling, or level of indispensability.

However, to achieve the potential of computer managed learning, a substantial burden will be placed upon users to specify required learning objectives; to prepare an inventory of knowledge resources (personnel, manuals, tapes, and so on); to develop modules of information including, where appropriate, audio-visual support material; to set up resource centres with terminals; to establish test banks; to appoint industry tutors; and to assess programmes and learning effectiveness.

It seems unlikely that any but the largest organizations would be prepared to 'go-it-alone' into an enterprise of this nature. Yet, there appears to be no escape from the necessity to accomplish these goals. It is clear that industry cannot dismiss the assistance which educators can offer, nor can educators remain aloof to the problems which industry faces in relation to maintaining competence of staff. Thus, a strong basis for collaboration between education and industry does indeed exist.

# References

Beder, H. (ed.) (1984) 'Realizing the Potential of Interorganizational Cooperation', *New Directions for Continuing Education*, Jossey-Bass, U.S.A.

Chesmond, C.J., Cook, H.P. and Miller, F.J. (1986) *Bridging the Education/Industry Communications Gap Through Joint-Venture Continuing Education and Training Modular Program Development*, Pacific Regional Conference on Electrical Engineering Education, Royal Melbourne Institute of Technology, Melbourne, December

Garry, F. W. (1986) *1985-1986 Annual Report of the National Technological University*, National Technological

University, Fort Collins, Co., U.S.A, p. 4

Miller, F.J. (1986) *A Comparison Between Adult Learning Preferences in Industry and Student Learning Preferences in Secondary School*, BEdSt Final Year Research Project (unpublished), University of Queensland

Miller, F.J., Cook, H.P. and Clark, C.Q. (1986) *The Use of Computers in the Maintenance of Workforce Competence*, Institution of Engineers, Australia, Electric Energy Conference, Brisbane, Queensland, 20-22 October

Stokes, E. (1986) *Pre-print Material for Institution of Engineers, Australia, Engineering Education Conference*, Topic 3 (Continuing Education), Melbourne, Victoria, p. 2, University of Queensland, November

**Thomas J. Ledwidge**, DipElectEng *Huddersfield Polytechnic,* BSc *Lond.*, PhD*Aston*, FIEAust, FInstP, CEng

Dean
School of Engineering
Darling Downs Institute of Advanced Education
Australia

**Frank J. Miller**, BEng(Elect) *McGill*, BEdSt *Q'ld.*, MIEAust

Senior Technical Training Consultant
Queensland Electricity Commission
Australia

Chapter Seven

CONVERGENCE IN PRACTICE AT GRIFFITH
UNIVERSITY[1]

Bob Ross

Griffith University in Brisbane, Australia commenced
undergraduate teaching in 1975. It has a very successful part-
time, undergraduate degree programme in its School of
Humanities. This programme is distinct in structure,
procedures and content from the School's full-time offering; it
explicitly incorporates a number of features of the distance
education mode and hence serves as a good example of
convergence in practice.

In this Chapter, I survey the history of decisions about
part-time study at Griffith University prior to the design of the
Humanities part-time programme. Other reports on the
development of part-time studies at Griffith University are
provided by Ross (1982), Barham and Buckridge (1983),
Buckridge (1984, 1985). I then describe some special features of
the programme, and finally I analyse some students' issues
arising from it.

---

[1] The ideas in this Chapter rely heavily on the work of the people who
have been involved in the part-time programme team and the students
in the programme. I am particularly indebted to my colleagues in the
Centre for the Advancement of Learning and Teaching who have been
most closely involved: Margaret Buckridge and Ian Barham, and in the
earlier work with the School of Australian Environmental Studies, Roger
Landbeck. In addition I owe a considerable debt to my former colleagues
at the Open University.

Firstly however, to put the discussion in this Chapter in context for readers, I will describe briefly the structure of bachelor's degree programmes at Griffith University, and provide some information on early planning decisions which preceded development of the Humanities part-time programme.

The basic academic divisions of Griffith University are called Schools. The bachelor's degree programme in all Schools has two main elements. A general foundation element occupies the first year of full-time study and a specialized main study element occupies the second and subsequent years of full-time study. Students must successfully complete the foundation element before they are permitted to enrol in the main study element.

The bachelor's degree programme is divided into semester units. Full-time students normally complete four units in each semester. One credit point is awarded for the successful completion of one unit. Students must accumulate twenty-four credit points to be eligible for the award of a bachelor's degree. The University specifies minimum rates at which students are required to progress through the bachelor's degree programme.

When Griffith University was being planned one of the important influences on the University was the presence in Brisbane (population around one million) of the University of Queensland. This institution is one of the largest universities in Australia and has both a large part-time, campus-based student contingent and a long-established distance education programme. Griffith University planners decided not to enter the distance education field but they did make a specific commitment to part-time teaching:

> Griffith University intends that provision for part-time study should be regarded as equally important a responsibility of the University as provision for full-time study ... .

(Part-time Students Sub-committee report to Student Affairs Committee. Subsequently ratified by Academic Committee, October, 1973)

This decision arose from the dissatisfaction being voiced by students in the programme at the time with the University of Queensland's part-time programme. The Griffith planners sought advice on part-time studies from part-time students at the University of Queensland, as well as examining a recent (at that time) report on part-time studies to the Board of Academic Studies at the Australian National University (1972).

One initial response of the Griffith University planners was to propose that:

> ... Griffith University should accept responsibility for part-time students but that some effort should be made to obviate distinctions between full-time and part-time students.

(Academic Committee minutes, April 1971)

This approach was replaced very early in the piece by the almost diametrically opposite view that:

> ... the part-time student is so different from the full-time student (e.g. age, motivation, objectives, approach to and time available for study) that arrangements made primarily for full-time students will normally be far from ideal for (part-time) students.

(Endorsed comment in the Report of the Education Committee, Board of General Studies, Australian National University, 1972, approved by Academic Committee, October 1972)

With hindsight, one proposition made during early discussions of the Academic Committee in March 1971 can be regarded as being prophetic:

> ... it might be possible to have only two classes of students - those in full-time attendance and those studying externally. Possibly there would be no advantage in providing for part-time students.

The University appeared to accept most of the advice it received from students in the University of Queensland's part-time programme, and an early meeting of the Academic Committee circulated a report which identified a series of problems that part-time students encounter and made proposals for meeting these problems. Among the proposals were that staff teaching part-time students should be given inservice training and have a lighter teaching load. The report recommended that there should be very few lectures and that most of the material should be presented by videotapes, notes, well-designed study guides and so on, with more emphasis being placed on tutorial teaching than is usually the case.

There was recognition of the work that would be required to design programmes that would live up to these aims. For example, the School of Science asked to be exempted for three years from the University's commitment to offer a part-time programme. The School's staff felt that the work involved in designing a common foundation programme for all students enrolled in the School would be jeopardized by simultaneous attempts to meet the goals set for part-time programmes.

The outcome of the ensuing debate was that only the Schools of Humanities and Modern Asian Studies offered part-time programmes in 1975, the first year of teaching. Sadly, these programmes were identical to the full-time programmes. Even more disappointingly the teaching procedures used were the standard full-time procedures but delivered at half-rate in the evening and at weekends. They showed little or no evidence of the University's commitment to part-time students. The Humanities programme received such a poor response that it was not offered for a second intake while the Modern Asian Studies programme, after a brief hiccup, has continued to the present, with some very successful students. However it requires a lot of support from the School's staff to keep it viable.

Discussion on part-time programmes was revived at the end of the 1970s, but this time the motive was considerably less altruistic. The proposals originated in the science areas of the University and were prompted by fears of falling full-time enrolments. During these discussions the Centre for the

117

Advancement of Learning and Teaching developed earlier suggestions for part-time studies in more detail. (The Centre for the Advancement of Learning and Teaching provides curriculum assistance and academic policy advice to the Schools within Griffith University. In addition the Centre is responsible for providing a wide range of audio-visual services for the University.) One of the documents submitted by the Centre reads:

## PART-TIME STUDIES

### 1.0 General Policy

*1.1 The University reaffirms its view that one of its functions is to make University education available to students who are unable to, or do not want to, attend the campus on a full-time basis.*

*1.2 The educational experience that the University, or its Schools, offers on a part-time basis should be consistent with the general academic goals of the University.*

*1.3 The University also reaffirms its view that, within the constraints imposed by 1.2 (above), the programmes it offers to part-time students should be designed, both in content and process, to meet the needs of and recognise the constraints on such students.*

### 2.0 Guidelines

*Within the general policy above the University would hope that any part-time programme would be designed so that as many as possible of the following requirements were met:*

*2.1 guidance in the form of lectures is not as prominent a feature as for full-time students. In place of lectures, relevant and carefully prepared notes, study guides and reading lists should be distributed;*

2.2 *failure in one course should not severely impede a student's progress;*

2.3 *students should be able to progress at different rates;*

2.4 *a given student should be able to progress at different rates at different times;*

2.5 *programmes should be coherent, integrated and interdisciplinary;*

2.6 *the amount of face-to-face information purveying should be cut to a minimum;*

2.7 *students should gain the maximum benefit possible from the time they spend on campus; and*

2.8 *the timetable constraints on student attendance should be minimised.*

3.0 *Most part-time students are likely to be mature students and the University would hope that any part-time programme would place some emphasis on developing students' ability to be self-directed learners and that the staff should see themselves more in the roles of guidance and resource persons than as information purveyors.*

('Part-time Studies' report of Steering Group to Academic Committee, September 1979)

A team from the Centre for the Advancement of Learning and Teaching and from the School of Australian Environmental Studies worked some of the ideas contained in the above document into a more detailed proposal (see below). However this extended proposal floundered, largely because of internal University politics. The School of Australian Environmental Studies then mounted a part-time programme consisting of a sub-set of its full-time programme, and taught in the traditional part-time manner. The programme was never very successful and ceased after four intakes.

During the same period the University's new School of Administration (as it is now called) initially offered its programme full-time in the evening with classes scheduled after 4.30 p.m. for a trial and then switched to a traditional part-time offering. The programme continues to attract considerable numbers of students even though this area of study is also offered on a part-time basis at three other higher education institutions in Brisbane.

## Developing Programmes for Mature Part-time Students

In 1979 a small team from the Centre for the Advancement of Learning and Teaching and the School of Australian and Environmental Studies tackled the task of developing a procedure that could be used to design a part-time programme for mature students. In part, this procedure was an extension of one proposed by Ross (1979).

These proposals were based on a set of assumptions about part-time students, their study patterns and the constraints they face. None of the assumptions was particularly new. They arose from the experience of the staff in the Centre for the Advancement of Learning and Teaching and from reports in the literature. They were confirmed by surveys of the limited number of part-time students already studying in the University (mainly in the School of Modern Asian Studies).

We assumed that part-time students were likely to be 'mature', that is, to have left compulsory education at least three years before joining the programme. They would be likely to regard their student status as secondary, that is their primary allegiance and responsibilities were likely to be elsewhere. Therefore there would be many demands on their time, other than study. Some of these demands will be hard to predict and will fluctuate in either a controlled or uncontrolled manner. Initially, many of these people will lack confidence in their ability as students and will have had little or no contact with higher education and its traditions and procedures. Most of them will bring wider experience to their study and they will generally be highly motivated.

From these assumptions we derived a set of features that we saw as desirable in a part-time degree programme: students should be able to study at times convenient to them and at a pace that suits their circumstances and their study habits. They should be able to break from their study for periods (a week, a month, a number of months, a year) without having to sacrifice the work that they have done previously. They should not have to waste their time in unnecessary activities.

These considerations highlighted a stumbling block to offering full-time programmes to part-time students at half pace. The Griffith University undergraduate degree programmes have as a major element a common foundation year for all students enrolled in each School. These programmes, which occupy a full-time student's first year of study, involve a coherent interdisciplinary study of all the areas of interest of the School. They are designed to give students a background to their main studies and to give them a basis for their choice of main study area as well as supplying the foundation on which later study will build. Students receive a single grade for successful completion of the foundation year. Under a traditional part-time approach students would have to complete two years of study successfully before they qualified for the award of any formal credit.

We wished to resolve this dilemma without losing the advantage of coherence and breadth of coverage in the overall degree. We realized that the foundation year already contained the basis for an appropriate structure. Each foundation year involves a number of assessment items. If we saw these as being linked in a sequence or network we could define a student's progress through the programme by the successful completion of assignments. Successful completion of each assignment could represent a recognized and defined stage on the way to a degree.

If, as well as defining programmes in this way, the 'teaching' was based largely on packaged material, students could be given considerable freedom to choose the pace with which they moved from assignment to assignment, where necessary breaking their study for periods to accommodate

121

their 'normal' lives.

The proposals for the design procedure developed with the School of Australian Environmental Studies are given below.

## PART-TIME STUDIES

*This is an attempt to illustrate a procedure that could be applied to the development of a part-time programme within a School.*

I        *Choose a descriptive title.*

II       *State broad aims for the programme.*

III      *Select ONE Main Studies programme from existing courses or parts thereof. (Pre-requisites are ignored at this stage.)*

IV       *For each course in the list ask: How does that course contribute to the aims?*

V        *Identify courses in the list that have pre-requisites that have not been included; analyse the nature of the pre-requisite; and propose possible action in each case. List the pre-requisite knowledge that cannot be incorporated.*

VI       *Expand the detail in the list by adding the main topics for each course.*

VII      *For each topic ask: 'Is this topic needed for the programme?'*

         *This questioning might result in the deletion of some topics, the identification of overlap in some areas and the possible insertion of new material.*

         *In the light of the restricted aims of the programme this stage might result in some shifts in emphasis and some increased integration.*

VIII   *This is the first stage in the design of the 'Foundation Programme'. We have already listed some material (in Stage V) that is 'needed but not covered' and so has to be included here. There are at least two ways of adding to this material:*

Either

VIIIA   *Identify the pre-requisite knowledge needed for the revised list of topics resulting from VII*

or

VIIIB   *Examine the present Foundation Course and select from it those topics that are needed to be able to treat the material in the 'Main Studies' programme resulting from VII.*
*In practice it would probably be advisable to use one of these procedures (VIIIB, say) and then check the resulting topics by using the other procedure (VIIIA, say). This stage would result in a list of topics that needed to be included in the 'Foundation Programme'.*

IX   *The 'Foundation Programme' would then be designed by 'fleshing out' the topics listed in VIII. This would be done with the minimum addition of material needed to produce a coherent development (or small number of developments). The result should be a rather 'thin' Foundation Programme. It will have been designed specifically to meet the needs of the selected 'Main Studies' Programme AND NO MORE. Frankly, the 'thinness' does not worry me at all. I am convinced that the way we are structuring the programme will mean that students will, in practice, do more work in the 'Main Studies' Programme than the average full-time student.*

At this stage we would have the full degree programme outlined with quite a bit of detail. By the end of Stage VII we should have started to abandon the 'boundaries' that enclosed the topics in the full-time courses we selected at Stage III.

X    Examine the total programme and set the topics out so as to show the developments and interconnections. At this stage completely abandoning the course boundaries that existed from Stage III. *(Obviously the original courses will still be more-or-less identifiable.)* This process might, again, result in a few deletions as we remove overlap or unnecessary material. It might also result in some additions as gaps in development or relationships become obvious.

We now have the complete degree programme, set out as one huge course, probably already showing a number of parallel 'developments'. The task now is to structure the programme in a way suitable for part-time students. There are a number of ways of proceeding from this point. In this example I propose to follow one procedure only.

XI    Return to the original courses that have been used to develop the programme. Extract from them the assessment proposals and insert the details of the assessment items from each course in the appropriate place in the final programme. My guess is that we would be inserting about sixty assessment items. At this stage we may have to devise an assessment strategy for the part of the programme that was originally the 'Foundation Programme' and insert the appropriate assessment items. In general this should not be necessary for the original 'Main Studies' part of the programme.

XII     *Examine each assessment item for*
       *. relevance to the programme*
       *. suitability for part-time students*
       *Both of these considerations might result in changes, deletions or additions.*

XIII    *Examine the total assessment package. Is the balance between types of item sensible? (e.g. too many/few essays/projects/ problems etc.) This might result in a few more revisions.*

XIV    *Set the whole programme out so as to show the lines of development connecting the assessment items.*

Comments

    *Students work by preparing the assessment items, following from one to another along the development lines. When students pass a particular assessment item they can go on to the next one on the 'development line'. A student who fails can immediately start to repeat the work for that item or continue work on another 'line'.*

    *The work for the assessment items becomes the course.*

    *Students are permitted to work at their own pace from assessment item to assessment item. (We will need progress rules specifying minimum progress rates in terms of assessment items.)*

    *Adopting this view of the course may suggest changes to some of the assessment items. As outlined above we would be requiring students to pass every single assessment item. This would require that we adopt a different standard of 'pass'; it would be preferable to specify the progress rules in terms of a maximum number of lesser levels of achievement, only insisting on a student repeating an item if it were awarded an 'unacceptable' mark (using a marking scale Excellent, Very Good, Good, Satisfactory, Unsatisfactory, Unacceptable). Even this would mean that not only would students be required to submit*

125

*every assignment but each would have to be at a level greater than 'unacceptable'. (A maximum number of 'unacceptable' marks could also be included in the rules.)*

## Some Questions, and Possible Answers

Q. *How would we give 'credit' to students with previous qualifications? (A liberal 'credit' policy is, in my view, to be encouraged.)*
A. *By specifying the assignments that each individual was exempted from.*

Q. *How would students know 'where they had got to'?*
A. *By seeing how many assignments they had completed.*

Q. *How would we describe a student's 'standing'? (To other institutions, employers etc.)*
A. *By reference to the original programme described in terms of full-time courses, mapping back by assessment items. E.g. 'Student X has completed the equivalent of Y.S.U. at an average grade of Z', the latter worked from mark levels using already existing procedures.*

Q. *How do we teach the course?*
A. *Within a very short time, students will be working on a range of different assessment items. Lectures clearly are of little use. Staff must see themselves more in a tutorial resource role. Specified times of staff availability could be arranged. Group tutorial sessions could be made available. Packages of learning material will need to be devised. The minimum resource would be a guided reading list. Workshop sessions around work for particular assignments could be a regular offering. Some material is already available, some could readily be adapted from existing material. The main roles of staff would be*

> *preparing and selecting material before it was*
> *needed and making themselves available to supply*
> *guidance and assistance at designated times.*

This procedure was not, in the event, used by the School of Australian and Environmental Studies but it was not long thereafter that the School of Humanities started to develop its own part-time programme and the foregoing considerations were relevant to this development.

## The Humanities Part-time Programme

Towards the end of 1980 the School of Humanities agreed that it should try again to offer a part-time undergraduate degree programme. The School accepted proposals from the Centre for the Advancement of Learning and Teaching that the programme should be separate and distinct from the Humanities full-time programme and should be specifically designed to meet the needs of part-time students.

Consistent with Griffith University's practice, a team was established to design the programme. One staff member of the Centre for the Advancement of Learning and Teaching was on the team. The procedure which was followed was that individual members of the team generated discussion papers that were then submitted to team meetings. This resulted in what must be one of the most fully documented planning processes ever. The structure and procedures to be used for the part-time programme were all developed before the content of the programme was decided, thus producing an interesting parallel with early planning, in 1974, of the School's full-time degree programme.

I (and many others) have claimed frequently that both the teaching procedures and the content of a programme should (ideally) be chosen to be suitable for the particular student audience. For example a 1972 report to the Board of General Studies at the Australian National University quotes the Ashby Committee on Birkbeck College London as saying:

127

> ... mature students should be taught differently from pupils straight from schools, and where possible even the content of courses should differ ... .

It is a relatively straightforward matter to find procedures for choosing suitable teaching methods for particular audiences: content choice is a rather more difficult matter. The Humanities part-time programme planning team explicitly discussed the appropriate content in these terms. Their success in attracting students suggests that they did indeed choose appropriate content in the area of Australian and Comparative Studies. When the part-time degree was launched this was not an area of major study in the full-time programme (there was a single elective unit). Its success as a part-time offering has resulted in the subsequent development of an Australian Studies major in the full-time programme.

## Development of the Programme

The task of developing the Humanities programme, then, was significantly different from the process that had taken place to develop the Australian and Environmental Studies programme in that the material was being planned rather than extracted from an existing programme. The programme was developed as a sequence of small units each of which would be assessed by one assignment (or examination). For successful completion of each unit students would be granted credit. There were to be forty-eight units in the degree so that each unit would be equivalent to about two weeks' work for a full-time student (about eighty hours).

As with the usual pattern of Griffith University degrees the first third of the programme was designed to be common for all students and to form a coherent introduction to all the areas covered in the total programme. In contrast to the full-time programme, where the foundation year consists of a single unit lasting a whole year, the part-time programme consists of sixteen sequential units.

The second third of the programme was designed to allow students a (limited) choice of emphases that they would give their studies - largely involving a choice of disciplines. The final phase of the programme (equivalent to the third year of a full-time degree) was to involve students in applying their disciplinary knowledge from the second phase to a number of case studies. This later became amended to 'applied study areas', still with much the same intent.

The sequential nature of the units in the first third of the programme meant that the students would be working on one unit at a time and would only face one assignment at any one time. Also the units were designed sequentially to achieve the coherence expected in a Griffith University degree.

To avoid a situation where students had to wait after the completion of a unit to get their 'results' before they proceeded to the next unit, the team decided that students would be allowed to proceed immediately to the next unit as soon as they had submitted the assignment for the preceding one. If the assignment for the completed unit did not meet the required standard, students were to be permitted to resubmit, after receiving advice. Students were to be allowed to be one submission 'ahead' of their results. For example if a student submitted the assignment for unit six and proceeded to work on unit seven, the assignment for that unit could also be submitted, but the assignment for unit eight could only be submitted after the student received a successful grade for unit six.

In line with the advice given them, the team decided to replace lectures entirely by packaged material and supplement this with tutorials, thus using students' attendance on campus in the most effective way by concentrating on group processes. It was felt that the tutorials have aims that are difficult to achieve in other ways whereas 'information purveying' and individual working with subject matter could be left to packaged material.

While tutorials for the programme were to be restricted to the normal semesters, the programme was arranged so that students could obtain the packaged material, work on it, and submit assignments at any time of the year, virtually allowing

129

twelve months' study time if they so desired. The turnaround of assignments submitted outside the full-time semester teaching period, however, was not guaranteed in the normal ten days maximum which is promised during semester.

In theory, students could work on their material at any pace and could conceivably complete the degree in two years (equivalent to full-time study for twelve months of each year). However, it was considered necessary to require a minimum progress rate from part-time students although this was set well below the rate necessary to meet the University's maximum period for obtaining a degree (ten years). The low minimum rate was to allow students to have a slow start in their return to study, whilst they built their confidence. Provision was to be made for students to take liberal breaks from study, even beyond the minimum progress rate.

One important early discussion in the team was about the form that the packaged material should take, particularly in the early phase of the programme. It was clear that the team would not have the resources to produce packages along the lines of the British Open University's materials, nor would the projected student intake of 150 per year justify the resources necessary to do so. The team decided to produce study guides to, and commentaries on, selected readings, making the selection of readings of critical importance. Only in limited sections, and only where absolutely necessary, was it going to be desirable to write a complete teaching package.

The team was clear that, at least in the early units, they needed to give students explicit assistance in developing study methods, including assistance in developing a range of reading skills as well as various types of writing skills. An awareness of these requirements in the development of the material was an important achievement. Unfortunately, ways of meeting them are still largely a matter of trial and error. Reliable prescriptions, at any but the most general and superficial level, do not exist.

The team was conscious of the frustration and annoyance that part-time students feel when they discover that the material they need from the library is not available because it has been removed by, or is being used by, other students. To overcome this, particularly in the early stages of the programme when many students would be working on the same material at the same time, the team made a decision to incorporate all the readings that students would need into the packaged material. This meant that there were no requirements in the early stages of the programme for students to attend the University library. However, this also meant that students were not, during that stage of the programme, developing the library skills so important in a Humanities degree. The team members were conscious that this ability would have to be developed later in the programme.

Face-to-face contact was to consist largely of tutorials together with an explicit recognition of the need to have staff available for individual consultation at times when students came onto campus for other purposes; mainly to attend tutorials, but also to submit assignments and collect packaged materials. The latter were to be made available through the University Bookshop.

Neither tutorials nor lectures are compulsory at Griffith University, and this rule seemed consistent with the intent of the part-time programme. It was thought, however, that many students would appreciate, or need, the opportunity to develop their understanding and ideas by group discussions involving a tutor. After some hesitation the team decided to identify sections in each unit that they thought would most benefit from group discussions and so arranged tutorials on particular topics or areas of each unit. In addition, the need to be able to respond to student queries on other aspects was recognized. Indeed, having made this decision the approach to the programme meant that some effort was made to structure the tutorials so that students would gain maximum benefit from attending.

Following this decision, the team was faced immediately with another dilemma: how to give students the flexibility to work at their own pace and still supply tutorial assistance at the point when it was most useful in each unit?

With the early tutorials this presented few problems: students would all be starting at much the same time. With an anticipated enrolment of 150 students there would be quite a

131

large number of tutorials on any particular topic and it should be a fairly simple matter to spread these tutorials over a period to cover most student progress rates. However the team expected that, as time from the common start (the same as the start of the full-time teaching year) increased the further apart students would be from each other in their studies. For the early units this problem could be accommodated by increasing the time spread for any particular tutorial and by allowing students to attend any tutorial session that they chose. It was recognized that, even with a reasonable spread of times for any particular tutorial topic, the tutorials would soon become a pacing mechanism. In addition to timetabling tutorial sessions to fit times nominated as suitable by students, and spreading them over a period to try to accommodate different progress rates, it was hoped that initially it would be possible to leave some sessions for each topic unallocated, and offer these sessions 'on demand'. That is, if a minimum number of students (five) asked for a tutorial at a particular time it could be held to suit them. There was a specific recognition that, for early units, the tutorials would need to be structured to assist students to develop their discussion skills.

Not surprisingly the team indulged in considerable speculation about the outcome. In general it was expected that there would be a group of 'high flyer' students who would move through the programme at an accelerated rate. It was clear that the first such group might push the production rate for the programme's materials to its limit. The compensation was that these students might well form an ideal 'trial' group for later units of material, working on it before it went to the final stage of production.

In general the team expected tutorial attendance to start relatively high and ease off as students gained confidence, and then to fluctuate as individual students found difficulty with different parts of the programme. In the long term it was assumed that tutorial attendance would reach a steady state.

## Issues Arising from the Programme

As with any programme that has been designed well in advance of its implementation, the team anxiously awaited the first enrolment figures. Even though most of the early material had been 'trialled' on potential students and revised on the basis of the trials, anxiety still existed about the reception the programme would receive from its students.

In the event, demand for the programme exceeded all expectations and remains high to this date. Intakes have been around the 250 mark; the fifth intake was at the beginning of 1987. The Humanities part-time programme has the largest student intake of any programme in the University. How has it lived up to the original expectations?

The programme has been remarkably successful. Its success can be judged on a number of different indicators:

(1) The programme has attracted considerable interest from academic staff in other institutions, both in Australia and overseas.

(2) After five years, applications for enrolment in the programme remain buoyant.

(3) The students in the programme are generally very pleased with it.

(4) The retention rate is remarkably high; one of the problems the programme design was attempting to tackle was the low retention rates in many part-time programmes.

(5) Students' success, as indicated by grades awarded, is very high.

However the Centre for the Advancement of Learning and Teaching perceives three categories of problems which overlap to a considerable extent. The three categories are administrative issues, student behaviour issues and academic

133

issues. Some but not all of these are accepted as problems by the University and the School of Humanities.

One apparently trivial administrative issue that has caused considerable hassle and has had a far from trivial impact is that of reporting numbers of enrolled students to our paymasters. As with all university courses, we are required to report student load to the Commonwealth Tertiary Education Commission as at April 30th each year. For full-time and 'normal' part-time programmes this exercise consists of counting (estimating?) the number of students enrolled in each course at April 30th and multiplying this number by the weight (in terms of the proportion of a full-time student load) of that course. These figures are then summed across all courses to give the student load.

In the Humanities part-time programme, students are only enrolled in one unit of the course at a time. Submission of an assignment automatically generates enrolment in the next unit. The usual procedure for reporting student numbers would result in a 'load' of between a quarter and a sixteenth of the appropriate figure. As the part-time programme team deliberately tried to allow for wide variations in student progress rates, it was very difficult to obtain a reasonable estimate of load, particularly in the early years. By now, of course, there are some historic data to go on, but as the team has been taking measures to try to improve the overall progress rate the load figures are still extremely 'soft'.

Load distribution of a different type has also added some constraints. The School of Humanities tries to even teaching load between staff and for a given staff member, over the year. While preparing courses (for which an adequate load allowance is made) is easy enough to schedule, the more the School allows students flexibility of assignment submission dates and offers tutorials 'on demand' the less control they have over the distribution of staff workload. Sadly this, together with the additional load on a hard-pressed administrative staff, has virtually eliminated the 'tutorial on demand' idea.

Student progress rates in the Humanities part-time programme have been just on the minimum rate. This was unexpected and is not acceptable. As explained earlier, the

134

minimum progress rate was deliberately set below the rate needed to achieve the University's maximum period for obtaining a degree. The team believed that, as with the 10-year period for full-time students, the minimum rate would be taken as just that. (In the full-time programme falling below the '10-year' rate is grounds for exclusion.) However it is clear that a significant number of these part-time students regard the minimum as the actual or desirable rate.

It appears that some students deliberately hold completed assignments until the last possible submission date, working them over to try to ensure they are as good as possible. (This behaviour also relates to the issue of the grades awarded and is discussed later.) While some students have achieved a good progress rate, the average has been on the minimum progress rate and the School has introduced further constraints to try to lift the rate without unnecessarily penalizing students returning to study. (A case could clearly be made for increasing the minimum progress rate after the first six to twelve months of study, while still allowing considerable flexibility in terms of variations between students and variations of rate with time for a particular student.)

In the first instance, the team toyed with the idea of getting students to indicate how quickly they intended to work through the programme and then hold them to that rate, with liberal provision to change the rate to adjust to circumstances. This was rejected, however, as being administratively too time-consuming.

Another behaviour that contributes to the unacceptable progress rates is that many students apparently wait for an assignment to be returned before starting the next unit in the sequence. In the first third of the programme, where units are all sequential, this means that students have nothing to work on while they wait for assignments to be returned. In other words these students do not take advantage of the facility that allows them to continue working on the next unit, and even submit its assignment, before they receive the results for their previous assignment.

In order to discourage this pattern of behaviour, the team has decided to try to encourage students to work on two units

135

at a time. In part, this is feasible because the linking between units has, in the event, been much less explicit in most cases than originally anticipated. In the second phase of the programme (the middle third), students study two different disciplinary sequences so they can be encouraged to have two units 'on the go' at one time, even though the sequencing in each string is tighter than in the first phase. In the third phase it is possible for students to work on more than one applied study area at one time, if they wish.

One feature of the programme that raises both administrative issues and behavioural issues is the pacing influence of the tutorials. The team was aware of the possible pacing influence of tutorials and attempted to lessen this factor in the ways described earlier. However one response to the unacceptable progress rates has been to reverse this attitude and deliberately attempt to use the tutorials to raise the progress rate. This response was in part encouraged by the recognition that some students stopped working through the package as soon as they got to the tutorial exercise (highlighted by using coloured sheets) and waited for a tutorial session to be held. The team is attempting to discourage this behaviour by decreasing the positive 'signalling', but is simultaneously trying to use this behaviour to increase progress rates by timetabling tutorials on a more limited range of dates, and earlier.

Another feature of tutorials that influences student progress is the tendency of some writers to incorporate material in the tutorials that adds to the package rather than merely complements it. This pattern is reinforced by the activities of some of the tutors.

Finally, let me return to the issue of the grades awarded. The behaviour pattern of delaying the submission of assignments to the last possible submission date has been one factor leading to the high level of grades awarded in the programme. There may, however, be other factors which should be considered in relation to grades.

The material in the programme is intellectually very demanding in places. In part this arises from the approach to learning that is prevalent in the School of Humanities. Put crudely, much of the material is rather abstract and 'second order' or 'meta' in approach. When this is combined with the students' behaviour in relation to the assessment in this programme some of us in the Centre for the Advancement of Learning and Teaching feel that there may be problems.

Briefly, the attitude to assessment adopted by the part-time programme team (largely on the advice of the Centre for the Advancement of Learning and Teaching) is that, particularly in this type of programme, the assessment items have a very strong influence on the work that students do. Taken together with the attitude that assessment items should relate closely to what you expect students to do with the material, this meant that the team placed a lot of importance on the design of assessment items. In addition the team made a conscious effort to explain to students what was wanted of them.

These factors combined with the printed and complete nature of the package lead to some suggestions that many assignments can involve a large amount of 'mapping' from the package, through the question, to the submitted work. To date the team is not convinced that this represents a major problem but, along with all other aspects of the programme, the Centre for the Advancement of Learning and Teaching is continuing to monitor and examine the issues.

In conclusion, the problems discussed here raise a number of issues that we in the Centre for the Advancement of Learning and Teaching think are posed by this programme. However, these need to be seen in context and should not detract from the undoubted success of this important innovation in part-time university education. There are useful lessons here for both distance education and campus-based programmes. It would have been surprising indeed if no issues had arisen from the implementation of this novel approach.

The question that remains with an innovation of this kind is: at what point should important characteristics of the programme be modified in response to difficulties which the team and students perceive?

# References

Barham, I. and Buckridge, M. (1983) 'Self-pacing in a University Degree Programme', *ASPESA Conference*, Darling Downs Institute of Advanced Education, Toowoomba, Australia, July

Buckridge, M. (1984) 'The Development of New Degree Programmes - Humanities', *HERDSA Conference*, Sydney, Australia, July

Buckridge, M. (1985) 'Assessment in Packaged Courses - Some Problems', *HERDSA Conference*, University of Auckland, New Zealand, August

Ross, R.A. (1979) 'Teaching the Same Courses Internally and Externally in Small Regional Colleges', *ASPESA Conference*, University of Western Australia, Perth, Australia, August

Ross, R.A. (1982) 'Part-time Studies: A New Approach', *HERDSA News*, **4**, 2, 3

**R.A. Ross**, BSc, DipEd *Syd.*, MSc *U.N.E*, PhD *Lond.*, FRSChem

Director
Centre for the Advancement of Learning and Teaching
Griffith University
Australia

Chapter Eight

# STAFF DEVELOPMENT NEEDS FOR UNIVERSITIES: MAINSTREAM AND DISTANCE EDUCATION

Ross Paul

Until recently, in Canada at least, there has been a clear distinction between mainstream, campus-based colleges and universities and institutions which employ the distance education mode. The most notable Canadian examples of separate institutions dedicated exclusively to distance education are Athabasca University in Alberta; the Open Learning Institute and North Island College in British Columbia; and the Télé-université in Quebec.

This distinction is apparently breaking down as distance education becomes more prevalent and more respectable world-wide. A number of reasons can be cited for this:

(1) In the Western world, and certainly in Canada, mainstream universities have been challenged by factors which are primarily economic and political. Increasing demand for a higher education has reached the point where governments are unable to provide the level of support necessary to meet the demand. Therefore, governments are designating funds for specific areas. This is a direct challenge to the traditional autonomy of universities. Within the private sector, the recognition of the importance of research and development in the face of international competition has led corporations to collaborate with centres of excellence and to expect more immediate returns on their investments in such centres than has previously been the case. The capacity of distance education institutions to take their product to the market-place puts them in a leadership position here, although they are frequently disadvantaged by the fledgling nature of their

research activities.

(2) In some cases the democratization of education to the tertiary level has combated the elitism of universities. Universities like the British Open University and Athabasca University in Canada have been successful and increasingly accepted as credible academic institutions by their mainstream counterparts. By virtue of their open-access policies they have been able to democratize education without sacrificing standards. However, there is great variety within any given cultural context. In countries with proud traditions of mainstream universities as highly elite institutions, distance education universities have the greatest difficulty achieving parity of esteem. One might, for example, cite the uphill struggle of Japan's Radio and Television University in this context. One way to achieve parity of esteem is to develop universities which democratize education but retain a strong commitment to academic standards and research. An example is Fernuniversität in Germany. (For a discussion see Mainusch, 1982.) In the developing world, the parity issue may not be quite as obvious, especially when one considers the large numbers of students enrolled in universities like Sukhothai and Ramkhamhaeng in Thailand, the Indira Gandhi Open University of India, and China's National Radio and Television University. However, such institutions do tend to serve an emerging elite.

(3) Universities are showing more interest in the mature student. In some countries the number of school graduates is decreasing while in other cases there is a heavy demand for professional upgrading and retraining. The demands of mature students are forcing changes in the traditional pattern of full-time attendance at daytime lectures.

A recent Canadian manifestation of the increased respectability of distance education and the pressure to respond to the growing demand for higher education in regional areas has been the creation of consortia of universities for distance education (the Open University of British Columbia scheme, the Maritime Universities in Eastern Canada, and the Manitoba Inter-Universities North project), which concentrate the delivery capacities and programmes of faculties from each of the member institutions to better serve isolated rural students, notably those in the north. The relatively high profile of these consortia and the fact that they encompass all of the mainstream institutions in a given region tends to accelerate the process of convergence. It is unlikely that many of these institutions would have shown much interest in consortia for distance education ten or twenty years ago.

These consortia are not the only examples of diverse institutions working together to meet needs that none of them could meet independently. Increasingly, institutions are working in close liaison to achieve ends that no single institution could. Athabasca University, for example, is seldom the 'whole' answer for a student, but is increasingly part of the answer in co-operation with other institutions near to where the student lives.

The focus of this Chapter is on the impact of convergence on the orientations, roles and activities of academics working in both mainstream and distance education universities. Much of the following discussion is derived from experience at Athabasca University which, uniquely in Canada, is a distance education university staffed, not only with instructional designers, but with a full complement of academics in each discipline. The University pursues the goals of open learning in the sense that students may enrol in any month of the year and any resident of Canada eighteen years or older may be admitted regardless of academic standing.

## Academics Working in Distance Education Universities

While the world of distance education is a burgeoning one, universities which are devoted solely to distance education have a fairly short history. This means that the majority of academics employed by distance education universities come from mainstream universities. This is the case at Athabasca University where only a handful of academics and administrators have had experience in distance education and where the majority of academics and tutors have graduate

141

degrees in the discipline they teach rather than in education or instructional psychology.

Those with no experience in distance education typically face a number of value conflicts and unanticipated problems in their new environment. For example, academics arriving at Athabasca University may face the following differences from their previous institution:

(1) There are no students on the campus.

(2) Teaching is not an individual's exclusive domain: it involves a long and complex course development process in which roles are specialized. Individuals must work closely with other academics, instructional designers, editors and/or visual designers.

(3) The demands of the production process may often be anathema to the mainstream academic's concern for professional autonomy.

(4) Athabasca's organization may be more highly integrated so that the services of the printshop or course materials distribution system, for example, are as important to the success of a course as any academic planning. This tends to break down traditional concepts of the 'academic' and 'support' or 'service' divisions of the institution.

(5) The product of the course preparation exercise is printed and available for all to review and to judge.

(6) Although academics retain primary responsibility for a course, it is usually a tutor, located outside the University, who has direct contact with students.

(7) There is no obvious beginning or end to the academic year - new students enrol at the start of each month, and there are no 'slack' periods when few students require attention.

(8) There are no classes to meet and therefore the rhythms of the mainstream university year are missing. Hence there seems to be too much administration and too little time for research.

(9) With no students on the campus and with colleagues working somewhat independently on their own course preparation and course presentation projects, there is not the same academic atmosphere or concept of 'campus' that provides basic socialization and stimulation to academics on a mainstream campus.

(10) Like Athabasca, many distance education universities were set up deliberately to be 'not like' mainstream universities and their founding members may find the influx of mainstream academics extremely threatening to the mission and style of operation of the institution. Hence, incoming academics may be surprised to find some colleagues opposed to such notions as the importance of disciplinary research, graduate work, or improving the university's reputation among mainstream universities.

The case may be somewhat overstated, but there is little doubt that the role of academics in a distance education university makes considerable demands on those new to the institution. Responses to these demands vary considerably from individual to individual. Some, notably those with a strong commitment to distance education and to responding to student needs, adapt themselves readily to their new environment. Others prefer to work somewhat independently anyway and are thus grateful not to face the interruptions of a more social environment. Still others manage to preserve their traditional roles, despite the new environment, by maintaining their commitment to research, meeting frequently with peers in other universities, and doing classroom teaching at night. However, some find the new environment very difficult and somewhat alienating. They typically go through a two or three year adjustment period where they compromise their role orientations to meet the demands of the distance education university and to 'survive'. This is most evident in their teaching and research functions.

## Role Conflicts in Three Major Areas

The role of academics at Athabasca University can be divided into three fundamental areas: research, course preparation and course presentation. Each area poses problems unique to distance education institutions.

### Research

The issue that best illustrates the conflicts experienced by academics working in a distance university is that of research. Perhaps because it is the hallmark of the mainstream university, research has typically been a contentious issue in distance education universities.

Typically, in the first few years of a university like Athabasca, the role of research is downgraded due to the pressure to produce a reasonable number of good courses in a short time. There is less emphasis on a disciplinary-based faculty, except in education and instructional psychology, and academics are hired more for their interest in teaching, their orientation towards students and their commitment to the values of the university than for their research and scholarship. Very quickly, however, usually in the interests of advancing the status and credibility of the university (so that its credits are accepted by all other universities, for example), and to meet the needs of the increasing numbers of academics who are oriented to mainstream education, the university pays more and more attention to the issue of research. Research credentials become more important in hiring decisions, contract negotiations produce terms and conditions which mirror the 'promotion through the ranks' system of mainstream universities, external examiners review scholarship in tenure and promotion decisions and in programme reviews, and the (typically) young academics view their scholarly output as crucial to their opportunities for promotion both within and beyond the institution.

Whatever their commitments to distance education, most academics at Athabasca continue to view research as crucial, both to their own success and to that of the University, a viewpoint that is extremely well presented by former Athabasca President, Stephen Griew (1982).

The most common complaint, one which Griew (p. 190) denigrates, is that academics in distance education universities do not have enough time for research. Griew argues there is no evidence that there is less time available for research in a distance education institution, but, at least in the case of Athabasca, it must be organized, or academics will find that the year goes by quickly dealing with course preparation, course presentation and management activities.

In this context, time management is a particularly important skill that may not always be associated with the preoccupied mind of a scholar. In mainstream universities, much time management is done for academics by the necessity to meet classes at set times, or to maintain regular office hours, and by the semester system which permits the allocation of major blocks of time for research in the summer months. The difference between mainstream and distance education universities is not the amount of time available but that its allocation to specific tasks requires more conscious attention in distance education universities.

Another interesting issue is the relative status of disciplinary and institutional research. The high student drop-out rates commonly associated with distance education institutions tend to result in preoccupation with research which seeks to evaluate the impact of various forms of course design and methods of presentation on student performance. This is also consistent with the principles of behavioural psychology on which such institutions tend to be founded. However, it conflicts with the emphasis on disciplinary research that characterizes mainstream universities. It may have an impact on the judgements of external reviewers who are assessing academics for promotion, or their value in a programme review, or for transfer credit.

The current trend towards more private sector involvement in universities is also posing a challenge to academic autonomy and disciplinary-based research. Distance teaching institutions may be able to capitalize on the increased private sector involvement in such areas as instructional design and inservice programmes, especially for manpower training needs, but they may be at a disadvantage because their evolution has not placed a premium on attracting top-rank research scientists. It should, however, be noted that small universities in general are affected by this concern, which is by no means confined to distance education universities.

## Course Preparation

While it has evolved towards a more pragmatic course-writing exercise involving course teams of two or three persons, Athabasca University's course-preparation activity, like that in most similar universities, still retains significant differences from mainstream course- or lecture-planning practices. The differences are significant enough to challenge the whole nature of university teaching and the role of academics.

At Athabasca the academic who is assigned to present a particular course may or may not be the course author. This role is frequently performed by external subject-matter experts, and another Athabasca staff member (an editor or instructional designer) may manage the course team. What is more, most of the direct contact with students is through telephone tutors located off the campus, often in regional centres. Nevertheless, in all cases, the academic is expected to retain overall responsibility for the courses in his or her disciplinary area.

Even when the academic presenting the course is the primary author, he or she will not have the same control over the process that is usually the case in a campus-based setting. The course may not be as elaborate as originally intended, because cost factors (such as printing costs, copyright, use of expensive media) limit ambitions. The course design may have been changed significantly by the instructional designer to respond to the needs and capacities of the University's part-

146

time adult students. An editor may have challenged the whole internal logic of the course or conveyed concerns about the academic's ability to write effectively.

Academics in distance education universities are also forced to pay much more attention to a phenomenon common to most teaching but seldom acknowledged very formally: the tendency to overestimate the amount of material that can be crammed into a single course. This is a problem especially for younger academics preparing a course for the first time. In classroom teaching, this lesson is learned over and over again, through poor results on mid-term tests, or lack of student response in discussions or to questions, which indicate that the students have not comprehended or lack the terms of reference which the academic had assumed. Cutting back on the original course plan, or even chopping whole topics out of the originally envisioned course, are common occurrences in mainstream university classrooms as academics adjust their expectations downward to those of the students.

The same phenomenon occurs in designing distance education materials, in that academics new to the field tend to be over-ambitious, especially because they know that the course materials will be available for anyone to scrutinize and they want them to be seen as professionally complete, thorough and credible. At the same time, they are forced (either by instructional designers or by poor experiences with the first version of the course) to anticipate the capacities of their students to cope with the materials and the independent study environment. The important difference from the classroom setting is the extent to which this adjustment must be conscious and carefully thought out in advance rather than as an impromptu response to the reactions of campus-based students. At its best, this is a highly stimulating process which produces collaborative excellence; at its worst, it produces something akin to the cynic's view of the typical product of a committee. The challenge for staff development is to achieve the former but the value-laden nature of this exercise renders this extremely difficult.

## Course Presentation

**Telephone Tutoring.** It is not only course preparation which forces introspection. Academics at Athabasa University are usually required to act as telephone tutors the first time that courses under their responsibility are presented. The challenges of responding to individual student needs over the telephone tend to encourage academics to examine their teaching styles and orientations more thoroughly than would otherwise be the case, and perhaps even at a more personal level than is usually possible in mainstream university classrooms.

The primary method of course presentation at Athabasca is the carefully designed and produced homestudy package containing all essential reading materials, which is augmented by a toll-free telephone tutorial service to any location in Canada. While the bulk of the responsibility for the telephone tutorial service is carried by the University's 200 part-time tutors, resident academics usually carry out some tutoring to maintain interaction with students and to monitor the effectiveness of their courses.

While the University produces a *Tutor Handbook* and has attempted a number of tutor training and development activities, there is little consensus, even among the tutors themselves, as to what should be the primary emphasis of their roles: counsellor, adviser, teacher, examiner, and/or friend. Telephone tutoring makes many diverse demands on tutors in ways that ultimately challenge individual philosophies of education and approaches to one's discipline. A common dilemma faced by tutors is how to reconcile the prevailing philosophy of adult education, which tends to recognize the individual as the best determinant of his or her learning needs, with their daily experience, which indicates that students lack the motivation, study or time-management skills or prior education to complete the course requirements.

**Seminar Support and Teleconferencing.** In the rural areas of Canada, in particular, students may have no option other than Athabasca University, but unlike the urban students who may choose Athabasca because of its self-paced independent mode of homestudy, they do not really want homestudy. Their strong preference is for face-to-face instruction and interaction with their peers. Athabasca's response to this has been to 'enhance' the homestudy packages with face-to-face seminars on a weekly basis or, if numbers are small, via teleconferencing.

In theory, this should be an ideal blend of the mainstream and campus-based modes, a primary example of 'convergence for excellence'. Students who come to the seminar or teleconference meeting have worked their way through the packaged materials, and hence they are free to participate in a lively discussion, applying what they have learned to the situations at hand.

In practice, this has frequently not been the case. Tutors may be frustrated by the rigidities of the packaged materials and they may be restricted in their ability to explore topics according to the needs of the students by central examination requirements. Tutors who are accustomed to autonomy in the classroom find it a major adjustment to be responsible for teaching materials prepared by someone else and to an examination which they may not have set. Also, it does not always follow that the homestudy package is as aptly suited to the seminar method of presentation. In particular, the more intensive pace of the seminar-support method may frustrate some students who are unable to keep pace with it, especially where the content is difficult and/or heavy.

## Staff Development Needs in Distance Education Universities

If one accepts the assertion that working in distance education universities poses a number of major conflicts for incoming academics who have not had previous experience in such a milieu, it follows that the institutions have a responsiblity to provide orientation and staff development programmes. It has been suggested that the adjustments faced by incoming academics confronted with highly integrated systems which challenge traditional notions of academic autonomy and freedom are major and that it takes a

149

considerable length of time for them to adjust to the distance education environment. At least in theory, the shock of this adjustment should be lessened by a well-developed programme which forces incoming academics to examine their own orientations and those prevailing in distance education institutions.

Some of the practical needs of such academics which might be addressed by a staff development programme are:

(1) Exposure to, and discussion of, the sorts of conflicts typically faced by incoming academics.

(2) Time-management seminars.

(3) Seminars and other interactive sessions focusing on instructional and institutional research and its implications for course preparation and presentation in the institution: student profiles, evaluations of various modes of delivery and student success rates, impact of pacing versus self-pacing, and so on.

(4) Workshops in instructional design.

(5) Feedback and strategy sessions on various ways of tutoring by telephone.

(6) Exchange programmes with other similar universities.

(7) Travel, professional development and research funds that encourage academics to visit other distance education universities and to develop their expertise in coping with their particular demands.

(8) Exchanges with mainstream universities to provide new academics with opportunities to test out their distance education ideas in the classroom and to maintain exposure to students and to peers in their disciplines.

(9) Discussion sessions which challenge traditional notions of research and discuss the importance of institutional research in a distance education university.

Although the emphasis above has been on the needs of academics and tutors, the same sorts of arguments could be made for several categories of professional staff, notably counsellors and other student services staff whose whole personal perspective is challenged by the need to counsel and advise students over the telephone rather than in person, or for librarians who never see the students they serve.

## Is Formal Staff Development the Answer?

To what extent can a formal programme of orientation and staff development reduce the tensions? Superficially, it would seem obvious that a programme designed specifically to sensitize academics to their new environment and to help them develop skills to cope with it would be beneficial. Staff development, however, is too often seen in quite formal terms by administrators anxious to produce neat and coherent programmes which lead academics to adopt certain orientations and practices, an orientation that tends to overlook the value-laden nature of the exercise. (For a more thorough analysis of the value conflicts experienced by traditional academics moving to an open university environment, see Paul, 1985.)

Instead of advocating a high-profile, formal, staff development programme, my preferred option is to suggest that the best professional development comes from the academic's own experience of preparing and tutoring his or her first course rather than from a special programme. While it may seem an abrogation of responsibility for a senior administrator to suggest this, the academic's own experience will ultimately be much more important in the longrun because of the large number of individualized variables affecting the success of such a venture, notably the demands of a particular discipline, the attitudes of the academic towards such basic tenets of course design as behaviourism and objective setting,

151

objective setting, the personalities of the team members, the budgets available, the timelines for course completion, the target student group and many other factors.

In short, this approach suggests that there is no 'one best way' to produce a course and that the academic's personal experience will ultimately prove to be the best staff development programme. This does not mean that there is no role for deans and other academic staff in all this. Of particular importance is the climate within the university and the sensitivity that is displayed to new academics when they first arrive. Peer support is particularly crucial when academics experience some of the conflicts outlined above. If, on the other hand, academics are left alone to figure everything out, they are in almost exactly the same position as isolated rural students. Campus-based university students know how tremendously supportive it is to find out that no one else in a class understood the lecture that day. Such support is unavailable to isolated rural students. Is there any reason to believe that it should be different for academics?

Where a supportive atmosphere exists, an exciting outcome is the impact of the experience of a distance education environment on the subsequent orientations and actions of academics. An example of this is the academic who works in an institution like Athabasca University for some time and then returns to a mainstream university. Inevitably, the academic finds that the distance education experience has had a considerable impact on his or her teaching. The discipline of breaking a course down into its smallest components and objectives and of tailoring it to the anticipated needs of the students (rather than doing this much more informally on a day-to-day basis in the classroom) has an outcome unanticipated by many academics: it changes their views of the course and how to teach it. It is perhaps the best example there is of the old adage, 'to teach is to learn'.

## Staff Development in Mainstream Universities

The convergence of mainstream and distance education is not a one-way street. Increasingly, academics in mainstream institutions are recognizing the value of instructional design, course team planning and the other requirements imposed by the alternative methods of presentation and the use of new technologies. As more and more mainstream institutions experiment with these methods, they are discovering impacts way beyond those originally intended. Academics who have authored distance education courses often find that they subsequently teach the same courses quite differently in a classroom.

The argument, here, then, is that the sorts of demands on, and activities of, academics in an institution like Athabasca are in themselves an important staff development programme, one that is guided by instructional designers, peers and course tutors. If one extends the logic further, then, an ideal form of staff development for mainstream university academics would be to participate in a course team at a distance education university, as a telephone tutor or in an academic exchange programme. While these experiences may not have been formally evaluated, they have an undoubted impact. In support of this, one could cite the testimonials of the many academics of other institutions who have written courses for or tutored at Athabasca University or the experiences of academics in Australia with 'integrated', dual-mode institutions of higher education. (For a discussion of the latter, see Jevons, Guiton, Foks and Knapper, 1985.)

It is important not to pretend that this is all brought about by distance education. Many university academics who have never heard of the term 'distance education' are actively pursuing alternative teaching methods, especially when interested by new technologies such as computer-assisted learning or interactive video-discs (Smith, 1985). Whether or not distance education was the original motivation, instructional design and its emphasis on meeting behavioural objectives, a hallmark of distance education, is ideally suited to the language and thinking behind a computer systems

153

approach to education. While many mainstream universities may be ahead in technological development in the 'hard' sense, distance education universities often have more experience with the equally important 'softer' concerns such as operationalizing instructional objectives and adapting the technologies to course presentation.

In conclusion, the convergence of mainstream and distance education universities is a clear trend, one that is accelerated by the accessibility of new technologies which can permit people to access every campus regardless of their location. The logical extension of this trend is a blurring of the differences between mainstream and distance education universities, especially as they work together to achieve common goals. One would hope, however, that each institution would retain its particular role within the system: the more elitist mainstream university catering to the graduate student and the distance education university serving the needs of the less advantaged student.

The argument here has been for recognition that both the mainstream and distance education universities have much to offer each other in terms of the professional development of their respective academics. Implicit throughout has been the assumption that specialization in one mode or the other is important if expertise is to be developed, but that such expertise is most valuable if it is shared in both types of institution and if every provision is made for academics to be involved in both modes.

Until recently, distance education universities have perhaps lacked the security to welcome such convergence with open arms. They have tended to emphasize their differences from campus-based universities and resisted tendencies towards mainstream orientations and staffing. It is argued here, however, that those universities are now sufficiently established to welcome convergence with a view to changing both mainstream and distance education universities into a new form of institution which benefits from the advantages of each. Given this approach, there is nothing wrong with staffing distance education universities with academics from mainstream universities or vice versa. As distance education

154

becomes more and more established, perhaps the mainstream universities will once again pay more attention to the teaching function and the needs of the students, to the ultimate benefit of the latter.

# References

Griew, S. (1982) 'The Neglected Role of Disciplinary Research in the Distance University' in John S. Daniel, Martha A. Stroud and John R. Thompson (eds.), *Learning at a Distance: A World Perspective,* Athabasca University/ICCE, Edmonton, pp. 188-91

Jevons, F., Guiton, P., Foks, J. and Knapper, C. (1985) 'Organisational Diversity Among Dual-mode Institutions', *Proceedings of the Thirteenth World Conference, ICDE,* Melbourne, Australia, Paper 1233, August

Mainusch, H. (1982) 'How Can the Conventional University Serve the Distance Learner?' in John S. Daniel, Martha A. Stroud, and John R. Thompson (eds.), *Learning at a Distance: A World Perspective*, Athabasca University/ICCE, Edmonton, pp. 187-8

Paul, R. (1985) 'Traditional and Non-traditional Values: The Politics of Distance Education', *Proceedings of the Thirteenth World Conference, ICDE,* Melbourne, Australia, Paper 1171, August

Smith, P.J. (1985) 'Distance Education: A Change Agent', *Proceedings of the Thirteenth World Conference, ICDE,* Melbourne, Australia, Paper 1012, August

**R.H. Paul**, BA *Bishop's*, MA *McGill*, PhD *Lond.*, PGCE

Vice President (Academic)
Athabasca University
Canada

Chapter Nine

STAFF DEVELOPMENT NEEDS IN DISTANCE
EDUCATION AND CAMPUS-BASED
EDUCATION: ARE THEY SO DIFFERENT?

David Sewart

Over the last two decades, developments in distance
education have spawned numerous attempts to define it. In an
effort to codify this mode of education in relation to
mainstream education, which is often called 'the traditional
method', a whole new terminology has arisen. Definitions of
distance education usually emphasize that it is distinct from
mainstream education. Also it is almost customary to point to
major differences in the skills required of distance educators
compared with campus-based educators.

In the writing of two prominent European distance
educators (Peters, 1973; Holmberg, 1981), we find attempts to
analyse ways in which this mode of education differs from
mainstream education. Peters described it as 'industrialized'
education because of the degree of fragmentation and
specialization of the teaching role which it engenders. He also
drew attention to the extensive use of technical media,
particularly in the creation of high-quality teaching materials,
such that large numbers of students can be taught at the same
time, even though they are geographically dispersed.

Basically Peters considered distance education to be a
method of indirect instruction, implying geographical and
emotional separation of teacher and student. Peters argued
that whereas in mainstream education the relationship between
a teacher and students in the classroom is based upon social
norms, in distance education it is based upon technological
rules.

Holmberg also begins his description of distance education by defining it as 'non-contiguous communication' thus emphasizing the lack of immediate two-way communication.

These theories do not rule out occasional face-to-face contact, but in neither is this contact explained. The overriding general emphasis is on the separation of teacher and student and the independence of the student in time and space.

In this Chapter, I argue that these distinctions may not reflect what is actually the case: distance education exists on a continuum of education which ranges from the totally teacher-supported to wholly teacher-unsupported, although neither extreme exists in practice. Moreover some distance education institutions appear to provide greater support to students than some mainstream institutions, particularly those in the higher education sector.

I claim that all teaching and learning is based upon the same fundamental principles. That is to say, there are certain general rules for learning and certain general rules for teaching. It is true that the applications of these rules might vary but there are no unique principles inherent in distance education which are not also inherent in mainstream education.

Whatever the method by which information is transmitted, learning can only be done by the students themselves. Certainly, some methods will be easier for the student, others more difficult. Likewise what suits some students may very well not suit others. Fundamentally the role of the teacher is to assist the student in assimilating and structuring information. In each teaching and learning situation a number of objectives are apparent, but the most important of these is related to the learning goals set for, or by, the individual student. To reach these goals the student will require suitable instructional materials and/or suitable teacher support.

Whilst not wishing to deny that a change of emphasis is needed in the transition from mainstream to distance education, I find it difficult to accept that the skills we see as necessary for teaching at a distance - two-way written communication, face-to-face tuition and student counselling - are of a different kind from those we associate with campus-based teaching.

If we consider the variety of teaching and learning processes that exist, we might place at one extreme the continuous face-to-face dialogue between one teacher and one student. This is a totally teacher-supported learning situation in which the student is wholly reliant upon the teacher in relation to both the content of what is being taught and the manner in which it is taught.

Further along the continuum we find the conventional primary school in which the authoritative figure of the teacher provides continuous contact for a group of students, but these students, being a group, learn also in relation to their peers. They can, if nothing else, begin to make a judgement of their own learning in relation to that of others, and they might also learn from those others.

Much further along the continuum we find the mainstream university teaching method in which the authoritative figure of the teacher appears occasionally - perhaps even rarely - and the students are, of necessity, more independent in their learning situation. In this case the instructional materials, normally books, take over much of the information conveyed by the primary school teacher, and peer groups play a much more significant part in the learning process.

At the far end of the continuum is the 'pure' method of teaching at a distance in which the students are learning at a distance from those who have prepared the instructional materials. They learn at their own pace, wherever and whenever they wish, and are often divorced from contact with fellow students.

## Distance Teaching Methods

The teaching in distance education falls somewhere between the extremes of a wholly teacher-supported and a wholly teacher-unsupported learning continuum. Precisely where is difficult to judge since distance teaching methods vary considerably in the way they are organized and in what they require of teachers. However, since the material through which the students learn is normally a highly structured predetermined package, it is clear that the distance education mode does not fall towards the totally teacher-supported end of the continuum. The distance education teacher is not the sole or even the most important agent for the transmission of what is being learnt, as is the case in the primary school; rather the facilitating aspect of the teaching function is highly stressed. Although from time to time the teacher might be called upon to supplement the information supplied by the package of materials, the emphasis is more strictly confined to explanation and clarification of the package, as well as encouragement and maintenance of motivation.

There has always been a beguiling temptation to assume that all the problems of teaching at a distance can be resolved by the production of a perfect package of self-instructional materials. The separation of course preparation and course presentation in distance education has led to hopes and expectations of this sort. It would be pleasant indeed if education could be defined solely as teaching since we would then start from a fixed standard package, entirely unified and controllable. It might then be tacitly assumed that the needs of the individual student could be subordinated to that package. Were this possible, we would truly have attained an industrialized method of teaching. Unfortunately - or perhaps fortunately - education is also about learning and there is a requirement to consider the needs of the individual student in relation to the package. This requires an almost infinitely variable approach, since the frames of reference of the students and their approaches to the teaching package cannot be stabilized within particular parameters. The distance education teacher is the mediator between the controlled package of materials and the infinitely variable student base.

## Adult Students Who Study at a Distance

In order to examine the role of the teacher in distance education compared to mainstream education I will look first at the students themselves, as it is their requirements which structure the teaching process to a large extent. In what ways are the adult students who are taking a degree or diploma from their homes and in their spare time likely to differ from students in mainstream higher education?

Sewart *et al.* (1975) summarized the needs of students entering the British Open University as follows:

> In its initial plan to create student support services through the medium of part-time staff based in local study centres, the University noted that adult education experience has shown that a substantial proportion of adult students' needs are non-academic in the strictest sense of the word. ( ... ) The experience of the Open University so far has established this initial assertion. What are these needs which differentiate the adult student from the conventional student for whom University education is the culmination of an unbroken linear progression which began in the nursery school? The needs are a direct result of his experience. On the one hand the adult student is concerned with the demands of adult life, with the concomitant social and financial pressures and with the maintenance of a place in a real community as opposed to the sheltered environment of the conventional undergraduate. On the other hand he is concerned with the objectives of what is being taught no less than with the content, with the consequences of his newfound wisdom upon his predetermined and ingrained sense of values no less than with the rationale behind that wisdom. (p. 7)

Adult students may be returning to education after a gap of several years. They may lack confidence in their ability to learn and, as a result, remain in constant fear of not doing well. Studies have shown that those with continued experience of learning as adults are the most successful in their adaptation to the new methods of learning which are the base of distance education, but even for these students the problem is not a simple one. Adult students in general have to develop concepts which demand new departures in thought and may not be compatible with, or at least easily be assimilated into, their previous experience. Adult students may have developed a very rigid framework into which their new knowledge must be set. The system of distance education, by definition, allows less contact with fellow students and an individual student may thus find it particularly difficult to define what 'doing well' really means and perhaps, therefore, even more difficult to establish reasonable goals and work patterns in relation to learning. Quite often students learning at a distance are studying part-time and their commitment to study may be difficult to define in terms of commitments to family and work.

In contrast, the students in mainstream higher education exist within a highly artificial framework. For the most part their study is merely a further stage in an unbroken linear development which began when they were in primary school. The infant class and the university tutorial are similar in providing a group learning situation and a subsequent possiblity of instant feedback of an oral and visual nature. The group learning situation offers a bench-mark to the individual members of the group.

All students may expect to fall short of the knowledge and understanding of the subject demonstrated by the teacher, but how far short is it reasonable to fall? The peer group provides a common denominator of achievement or failure for all its members as well as allowing interaction between its members in relation to the academic content of the course and thus providing an alternative, albeit far less formal and far less reliable, than the teacher.

So far we have looked at negative factors for students in distance education. Are there are any positive factors? Most important is motivation. Students in distance education have to make an individual and conscious decision to study by this mode. They have to offer commitment and they do so on the basis of an experience that is almost certainly broader than that of campus-based students. They usually offer that commitment with firm objectives in view, objectives which might sometimes be purely personal in nature, might sometimes be vocational or might be a combination of both.

## The Teacher in Distance Education

What then can we say about the role of the teacher serving distance education students? In mainstream education the teacher is the 'face of the institution' but many distance education institutions have divided up the role of the teacher. Whereas in the campus-based education system, the teacher is responsible, to a very considerable extent, both for the preparation of what is taught and for the presentation of what is taught, in distance education a clear distinction is drawn between the two elements. In many large distance education institutions there is a complete division of labour in preparation and presentation.

### Preparation

Course preparation normally involves the creation of a package of attractively presented self-instructional materials. Printed material invariably forms the basis of this package but it can be, and often is, supplemented by audio-visual material either in the form of cassettes, transparencies, or open circuit broadcasting. Sometimes too, home experimental kits are included as part of the package. Customarily a great deal of thought is put into the assembly of this package and it is made as attractive as possible for the students. Often, the package is the compilation of the work of a number of people: a course team, which might include editors, designers and producers as well as academic staff. This package is then transmitted to the students and forms the basis of their learning.

### Presentation

Presentation of the package may take place in a number of ways: through local face-to-face contact with the student or by the various means of communication at a distance such as telephone, mail and so on. Sometimes the teacher responsible for the preparation of the material might also be involved in the presentation of the material. This is not essential, however, and the essence of the total process is that preparation takes place through one or more people in the distance education institution, and presentation can take place for a student at a distance from the institution through the agency of a totally separate individual or group of individuals taking on this element of the teaching function.

The separation of the functions of preparation and presentation is usually highlighted as the feature which distinguishes distance education from campus-based education. But is this really the case? It is true that the primary school teacher embraces the functions of preparation and presentation but it is certainly questionable whether this occurs throughout all levels of mainstream education. In higher education the teacher, whether offering a lecture or a tutorial, is likely to be offering a presentation against a background of recommended reading, set books, library research. In other words, in higher education the presentation aspect almost invariably assumes additional resource materials and the presentation is designed to fit in with these resources.

Is then the separation of preparation and presentation a distinguishing feature of distance education? Surely not, if we accept that this separation also occurs in mainstream higher education. Have we, therefore, identified another continuum in teaching with the complete integration of preparation and presentation by one individual at one end, and the total separation of these functions at the other? On such a continuum, distance education would be clustered towards the 'separation' end, but there would be a wide variation depending on the particular institution with perhaps some of them less close to the 'separation' end than in mainstream higher education.

There might still be those who point towards a generic difference in the total teaching process for distance education. It might be suggested that in mainstream education the teacher making the presentation has control over the elements of presentation and resource preparation because the resources, in terms of set books and so on, can be defined by the teacher. The same is not true in some distance education institutions where the resources are entirely circumscribed as far as the presenting teacher is concerned and the presentation is wholly subservient to the resources which have been previously defined for students and presenters alike. Here too, however, I would hesitate to see a generic difference between distance education and mainstream education. The teacher-presenter in distance education is not making - indeed cannot make - a presentation wholly circumscribed by the package of materials. Teachers making presentations do so from the framework of their own relevant knowledge and learning experiences. It is their own knowledge and experience which allows them to act as mediators between the resource package and the students. They might be more dependent on the package than teachers in mainstream higher education but they are not wholly dependent on it. If this were so, there would be no point in having them there at all as they would be identical to the package itself.

## Teaching Skills

We have looked at the student in distance education, we have looked at the elements of preparation and presentation and at the role of the teacher in distance education in relation to these. We can now move on to define the skills required amongst teachers engaged in distance education. Is their training to be different from those of mainstream teachers and, in general terms, can we say that a different sort of person is required for distance education? Not all of the requirements for teachers in distance education will be needed in each case, or in the same measure, but a reasonably comprehensive list will form a suitable basis for trying to answer the question.

### Two-way Written Communication

Two-way written communication is the central teaching method in distance education. The techniques and approaches of the teacher, sometimes called the correspondence tutor, are not always immediately apparent to those engaged in campus-based education, just as learning at a distance does not always come easily or naturally to the students who, almost

164

invariably, have an experience of education strictly delineated in campus-based terms.

The way in which students perceive their relationship with their teachers will influence considerably the way in which they respond in terms of their written work. If they perceive the relationship as one of strict authority on the part of the teacher, their attempts to be individualistic and explorative in presenting ideas within the framework of their previous experience will be severely limited. It will follow that the educational value of their written work will be minimized and its role as a grading instrument will become its most important or even perhaps its sole function.

Moreover, the students' initial experience of written assignments is likely to be an enduring one and will colour their future attitude to this activity. It is therefore of considerable importance that, from the start, students should use assignments as vehicles for exploring knowledge within a particular framework and receive guidance which will assist them to explore along coherent paths. That is not to say that a written assignment cannot be used as a grading instrument. Assignments are used extensively for grading purposes in distance education but the approach of the teacher is all-important. The role of teachers must not simply be that of grading, nor even simply of correcting or redirecting: they must look to what is best in their students' work and start from the basis of reinforcing this.

The concept of the teacher as 'mediator' between the material and the student is widely established. This role is nowhere more apparent than in distance education, and particularly in two-way written communication, where the content and demands of the learning materials may be divorced from the students' frame of reference. In distance education therefore, the teacher has to adapt the needs of the individual student to the material, and vice versa, and to do so - or at least to do so successfully - the teacher must have the ability to convey advice through the comments which are made and the ability to grasp the student's level of knowledge and conceptual framework. The latter indeed is an essential requirement if the advice is to be seen by the student as relevant.

I have already referred to the separation of preparation and presentation in distance education. A carefully constructed package of materials, attractively presented, might be interpreted by the student as entire in itself, a sort of academic pabulum which, once consumed, will provide the perfect everlasting nourishment. A teacher has to overcome such simplistic concepts on the part of the students. Students have to be brought to a relationship with a package of materials which is critical and independent. They must not be allowed to assume that the package, because it is so well constructed, is 'right', is 'the answer' or contains within it all that can be known on a particular topic. What must be avoided at all costs is a slavish dependence on the package which, having once been ingested, need only be regurgitated to demonstrate a knowledge of the subject.

An essential element of the learning process in higher education is the clash of opinions, the challenging of concepts, and the questioning in relation to a particular framework. This is no less the case in teaching at a distance but the manner in which this is done must be different, given the normal perception of the written word as weighing more heavily than the spoken word and given the isolation of the student in terms of any peer group. The same thing may be said of statements made by those responding to assignments and other written work in terms of clarity of meaning and likely comprehension by the student. The written word is totally lacking in the inflections and gestures which are so much part of the face-to-face method. Consequently it requires far greater clarity if it is not to be subject to misinterpretation.

## Face-to-face Tuition

Written two-way comunication is central to distance education but it is not the only method of presentation employed by most institutions. Face-to-face contact at residential schools, evening and weekend classes is also very common and an integral part of distance education in many cases. Confusion often arises however, because, while the residential session is apparently identical to the campus-based experience of teaching and learning, in fact it entails some differences in approach. Unfortunately, it is often the case that face-to-face contact in distance education is equated in the minds of students with the mainstream teaching methods with which they have been accustomed. While face-to-face contact does not necessarily embrace the entire formal dissemination of information in mainstream education, it nevertheless contains significant elements of this, whereas in distance education the package of materials embraces the major part of the information.

Face-to-face tuition in distance education is therefore more restricted in its objectives. It might be seen sometimes as remedial, sometimes as supportive, sometimes as interpretative. The teachers' role is not to introduce new material but rather to see that students comprehend the ideas within the teaching package which they have already received, to remedy academic weaknesses discerned in relation to the package and to mediate between the package and the individual students.

Of course the presentation element of teaching in distance education may use other methods than face-to-face contact or written communication. Many systems of teaching at a distance now employ telephone contact extensively, and we are moving into an era of links through on-line computers. The role of the teacher, however, does not change radically with the medium of communication at a distance. A particular ability, such as keyboard skills, may be useful or even perhaps essential for a specific medium but the underlying role of the teacher in teaching at a distance does not change.

## The Counselling Role

The British Open University is often held up as a shining example of student support services in distance education but it is notable that, whereas in theory it had recognized the need for this support before its first intake of students, it was not until 1976 that it had adopted a practice which wholly embraced this theory.

167

Commenting on the roles of tutor-counsellors at the British Open University Sewart *et al.* (1975) wrote:

> By linking each student at foundation level to a tutor-counsellor and by continuing this association beyond foundation level wherever possible the Open University has sought to meet this discerned need by providing a continuous educational support which cuts across disciplines and across Faculties. The frequent contact, whether by face-to-face or by other methods, the subject link which is reinforced through the correspondence element and the provision of sympathetic assistance in the formulation of a constructive, efficient and beneficial work pattern within the novel institutions of the Open University system, all these serve to provide a sound basis of interaction and mutual understanding between student and tutor-counsellor at foundation level on which the student can build and rely in the course of his later studies. It is this relationship which breaks down the isolation of the home-based learner and begins to encourage and shape the effective dialogue which is the basis of the educative process.

> The Open University student probably has more freedom and more choice in his degree profile than any other student. This freedom, however, in turn demands of the individual student a number of important decisions which would normally have been made for him. It is an interesting and perhaps sometimes infuriating paradox that this provision of flexibility to cater for individual needs inevitably results in increasing complexity of administrative and organisational procedures which may present the student with problems. The tutor-counsellor must be able to assist the student in this complex teaching and learning environment. (pp. 8-9)

The above was written in 1975 in order to explain the need for general student support services in an 'industrialized' mode of education which was at least as complex as anything which had been attempted at that stage. But was it really asking for new skills for those who were to act as tutor-counsellors in the British Open University? Is this counselling function unique to distance education? Is it indeed a skill which arises wholly from the nature of distance education? Clearly that is not the case. There have been a number of major changes in mainstream education in the last two decades. The whole scale of higher education has been enlarged and this has certainly made students more remote from their teachers and probably also from one another. Forms of educational technology, which are increasingly machine-based, have been developed and introduced on a wide scale. The social base of the student population has broadened while the curriculum has not seen such dramatic changes. Students' expectations have become more diversified and the relationship between education and vocation has been intensified. There have been further moves in society at large away from the family and its close supportive relationship. Specialist knowledge is expanding and, at the same time, all knowledge has become less permanent and more liable to amendment or even radical revision. Mainstream higher education has, in this period, become more depersonalized and students have become alienated from their tutors and institutions. Mainstream education has sought to combat this through the provision of people it has called generalist tutors, mentors, or counsellors. This role and the need for it exist no less in mainstream than in distance education.

In 1975 the British Open University was defining the need for tutor-counsellors to help students faced with their relationship with a distant and complex institution. As such it was not identifying new skills but highlighting elements which have traditionally been a part of good teaching, namely an appreciation of the students in the environment in which they are learning and hence the sympathetic support for them.

We have seen that in the written communication and face-to-face methods, differences between distance education and mainstream education may be discerned, but these differences are no greater than amongst mainstream methods of education. Here teachers are not just concerned with providing a curriculum and teaching that curriculum. They have a broader educational and counselling role in relation to their students. This too is a part of teaching at a distance. The teacher in distance education has a generically similar function to the mainstream teacher. All teaching arises from the content of what is to be taught, the curriculum, the support to students relating to the strictly academic content of the course and the general support to students arising out of their broad educational needs. We may posit a continuum for each of these three elements, and distance education, like all other forms of education, will appear on each continuum. It will not be at the extreme and it will normally fall within that band of the continuum in which are found the mainstream systems of higher education.

## Staff Development Needs in Distance and Mainstream Education

If this is the case, are there any requirements for training or staff development for those involved in distance education? Yes indeed. Staff development should help to highlight the different stress placed by distance education on specific elements of teaching. In this sense, however, it will be institution-based since it will assume a background of theory and general good practice and build its particular requirements onto this. Unfortunately, however, in higher education in Europe and in most other parts of the world, such an assumption is invalid. Teachers in higher education have not had the benefit of specialist teacher training or more general staff development programmes.

Until recently there has been a prevalent assumption in universities in the United Kingdom that teaching in higher education is not something for which a training programme is required. Indeed, whereas in primary and secondary education prospective teachers are normally required to have completed a course before they take up a post, only in Eastern Europe is this true of higher education. Thus training in higher education is normally an inservice activity - on the assumption that it exists at all - but the term 'staff development' is a broader concept than 'training' and is of more recent currency. It does not embrace pre-service courses since the 'student teacher' cannot be seen as a member of staff, but rather encompasses inservice training of various types. In higher education in the United Kingdom training programmes have concentrated mainly, or even exclusively, on the general improvement of teaching methods. Such programmes appear to assume an agreed generalized good practice for teaching across all disciplines. This is not staff development. The needs of teachers in different subject areas will differ. Moreover teachers will be approaching teaching from different backgrounds. Their knowledge of pedagogy will differ, as will their knowledge of educational technology. Staff development is concerned not only with teaching good practices, it is concerned with creating a harmony between the individual and the institution which allows the commitment of staff to be maintained within the aims of the institution. It is concerned with the context of the institution, the subject which is being taught, and the individual teacher, as well as general teaching techniques and strategies.

The basis of inservice training for university teachers in the United Kingdom has been courses on the theory and practice of lecturing. This is probably not at all inappropriate since new entrants to the profession normally demonstrate an inordinate anxiety about publicly presenting or exposing themselves as experts on a topic before a large audience. The campus-based lecture embodies an outstanding paradox in that, while the lecturer and students are obviously linked very closely in physical terms, there is an apparently unbridgeable gulf in their relationship. The lecturer speaks, the audience listens. The lecturer is the expert, the audience mere students. The lecturer presents what he or she wants and in his or her own preferred manner, the audience has no opportunity or right to comment. Not surprisingly, this inservice training in 'lecturing' is normally offered in the form of a lecture and thus the method of presentation reflects the course content.

Lecturing is only a part of campus-based teaching, as we have seen. It is generally agreed that people learn by 'doing' rather than by listening passively. It is appropriate therefore that staff development should employ methods appropriate to its content. It is here that the practices of staff development in distance education can perhaps combine with the emergent staff development in traditional tertiary education.

The British Open University is alone amongst the large-scale teaching institutions in possessing a reasonably coherent staff development policy for the many part-time staff (about 5,500) who provide the teaching and counselling for its students. The practice of staff development is, to no small extent, in the image of the institution's study system in that printed materials, broadcasts and face-to-face meetings are used. Yet while this policy embraces teaching methodologies and is concerned with an individual's teaching in relation to the aims of the institution, it is not consciously concerned with the development of the individual. It approaches the harmonization of the individuals' and the institutions' goals from a purely institutional standpoint. There are a number of reasons for this. The staff to whom the policy is applied are part-time employees. While many are, in their full-time posts, teachers in higher education in the United Kingdom, only a proportion have been engaged in staff development or training activities in that full-time role. Moreover teaching at a distance is 'unconventional' and there is a need to explain distance education to those who are to teach in this mode without ever having been distance education students themselves.

In conclusion, let us reiterate our comparison of distance education and mainstream higher education. From this comparison it appeared that there were no generic differences. Moreover while large-scale distance education institutions tend towards a division of labour between course preparation and course presentation, this is not the case in other systems of distance education, notably in Australia. We have seen a generic similarity in the elements of mainstream higher education and distance education. The differences are no greater than those usually discerned between primary, secondary and higher education. Similar differences exist amongst distance education institutions themselves. It is appropriate, therefore, to look at staff development in distance education in close association with staff development in mainstream education, and more particularly so since a growing proportion of staff are engaged in both, either in the so-called 'integrated' Australian institutions or in dual employment, working full-time in one mode of education and part-time in another.

Developments in distance education over the last two decades have emphasized the needs for training in particular aspects of teaching, but these are not generically different from mainstream teaching, they merely show a change of emphasis arising from organizational differences in distance education. Inservice training is a relatively novel concept in most higher education institutions. Staff development is even more novel. It is a term which has been used in commerce and industry, the civil service and the armed services, where it has been associated with management training. It is, as we have seen, far broader than 'teacher training'. If it is to meet the needs of the individual rather than concentrate on the teaching of methods, it must recognize the varied array of teaching-learning organizations which now exist and with which teachers will be variously concerned from time to time in their careers. These are referred to variously as mainstream education, distance education, open learning, continuing education, and so on. Many of them relate to defined categories of students and require slightly different methods from those which we understand as mainstream teaching. However, they are all, in reality, points on the same continuum. A coherent staff development policy in higher education must not only acknowledge, but embrace the whole range of educational provision which is now available at that level.

# References

Holmberg, B. (1981) *Status and Trends of Distance Education,*

Kogan Page, London, p. 11

Peters, O. (1973) *Die didaktische Struktur des Fernunterrichts. Untersuchungen zu einer industrialisierten Form des Lehrens und Lernens*, Tübinger Beiträge zum Fernstudium 7, Beltz, Weinheim

Sewart, D. *et al.* (1975) *The Roles of the Part Time Staff in the Open University*, The Open University, Milton Keynes, pp. 7-10

**David Sewart**, BA, PhD, *Leeds*

Director
Regional Academic Services
The Open University
Milton Keynes

Chapter Ten

# BARRIERS TO CONVERGENCE IN AUSTRALIAN HIGHER EDUCATION

Mavis Kelly

In recent years, distance education has been heralded variously as a unique form of education (Keegan, 1980), a new academic tradition (Shaw and Taylor, 1984) and a radical challenge to the concept of a university (Rumble and Harry, 1982). To a large extent these claims ride on the success of the British Open University and other national institutions which teach only at a distance. These institutions are frequently characterized by open entry, use of technology in the preparation of course materials, and use of public broadcasting. Institutions of higher education which teach at a distance in Australia are not of this type: campus-based and distance education modes co-exist in the same institution.

At first glance, it might appear that convergence of distance education and mainstream education would be achieved fairly readily in institutions where both modes co-exist. Indeed the Australian system is frequently described as 'integrated': and it is integrated, but only in the sense that there are no separate departments consisting of academic staff who teach only at a distance. The same academics are responsible for both campus-based and distance education students.

Both campus-based and distance education have much to gain from fuller integration in terms of expanding the range of courses available to distance education students; economizing on teaching functions; allowing campus-based students greater flexibility in choosing from a range of resources and strategies for learning; and in the case of part-time, evening students,

175

removing the necessity of regular campus attendance. Moreover, in a dual-mode institution there are the advantages of allowing academics to maintain contact with colleagues in their discipline, to benefit from contact with postgraduate students and to continue to work in a research-oriented environment.

While cases of successful integration or convergence in dual-mode institutions do exist, for example in several Schools at Deakin University in Victoria and the Humanities part-time programme at Griffith University in Queensland, these are by no means prevalent.

In this Chapter, I highlight some barriers to convergence in dual-mode higher education institutions in Australia and suggest ways in which these might be overcome.

In the first instance, I look at some major institutional barriers to convergence: administrative structures including costing and funding, staff workloads and academic promotion systems.

Staff and student perceptions of the different modes of education are also examined.

Finally, I examine barriers put up by the government agencies that are responsible for developing a national overview of higher education and for long-term educational planning.

My analysis is derived mainly, but not wholly, from the Australian situation. I am convinced, however, that it has substantial relevance in other countries where dual-mode institutions exist.

## Institutional Barriers to Convergence

A number of institutional variables create barriers to the convergence of distance education and mainstream education in Australia.

(1) In all higher education institutions which offer distance education courses, the distance education component has been grafted onto traditional administrative structures devised originally to cope with the needs of campus-based education. The outcome of this grafting process is that administrative

structures which serve a campus-based educational system are inadequate to serve distance education programmes.

(2) Academics who teach at a distance bring with them a set of values, attitudes and skills which are not always relevant to the distance education mode.

(3) There is some evidence to suggest that a high proportion of students studying at a distance would prefer to study in the campus-based mode if they could, and that they also tend to be conservative about the possibilities of using technology for teaching and communication. It may be that this preference is related to the low status of distance education in Australia for most of its history and to the relatively pedestrian methods of course preparation and teaching which existed until quite recently. Campus-based students can also erect barriers when confronted with innovations in teaching which are designed to encourage them to adopt a more independent approach to learning, for example in the introduction of resource-based teaching.

## Administrative Structures

There are three primary administrative barriers to convergence of distance education and mainstream education in dual-mode institutions: costing and funding systems, methods of determining academic teaching loads, and systems of academic promotion. At a time when government spending on education is severely limited and mobility and academic promotion are restricted, these factors work together to rigidify existing structures.

**Funding and Costing.** Intra-university resource allocation is largely an autonomous process but as Guiton (1982) points out, overall recurrent funding focuses on a number of cost factors: staff/student ratios; staff contact hours; and weighted student units.

Several studies have shown that the costing of distance education is radically different from that of mainstream education, principally in the proportion of recurrent costs associated with course preparation: these costs are fixed rather

177

than variable in relation to student numbers. In dual-mode institutions it is rarely the case that formulae for allocating budgets to teaching departments and to distance education sections are altered to accommodate the actual costing of distance education.

As Guiton (1982) and Rumble (1986) suggest, a more intelligent formulation for recurrent expenditure in distance education would be allocation of funds on the basis of: course-related costs (fixed costs); student-related costs (variable costs); and institutional costs.

The ratio of staff to students, which represents variable costs, is an inappropriate basis for assessing academic teaching efforts in distance education. Likewise, number of face-to-face contact hours is meaningless as a measure of workload.

Under current funding procedures the usual strategy is to ignore some of the course-related costs of distance education: principally the time needed for academics to prepare and revise courses. This will be the same regardless of whether an academic is preparing a course for ten or one hundred students. Associated with this is the cost of employing non-teaching professionals to assist in course preparation and the minimum infrastructure required to maintain a distance education operation of any kind.

In single-mode distance teaching institutions, it is usual to justify these high fixed costs by enrolling a large number of students in relatively few courses, thus reducing the cost per student head. The British Open University is a prime example of extremely high fixed costs spread over a very large number of students. This is combined with prolonged 'shelf life' of courses, enabling course costs to be annualized and hence reduced.

The dilemma in Australian higher education is that government funding is provided to dual-mode institutions on the basis of mainstream costing. To change or complicate categories of funding implies risks of which many distance educators are aware. See, for example, Griew (1980) for a discussion of this issue.

Within a dual-mode institution, administrators who wish to suppress distance education in favour of mainstream activities can use the strategy of refusing to recognize alternative costing systems even though those that are being applied are patently wrong.

For example, suppose an institution has budget line categories of: staffing and maintenance; equipment; and research.

Within a distance education infrastructure many activities must be included under maintenance that would not be present in mainstream teaching: costs of printing and mailing materials for example. This greatly inflates this part of the budget compared with other departments in the mainstream sector of the institution. Likewise there will be a number of staffing positions, both clerical and professional, which are not found in mainstream departments. The distance education section may then be called on to justify a high staffing and maintenance budget compared with mainstream departments rather than in comparison with similar distance education sections elsewhere, which would be the appropriate basis for comparison.

These costing problems will become apparent also in mainstream departments which may use some distance education methods. At the very least, they will encounter printing costs that have not previously been incurred as well as fixed costs associated with course preparation. Alternatively, course preparation will become an additional load carried by academic staff members, as is frequently the case in distance education in many institutions.

Unless a department can attract generous funding from outside sources to cover these costs, the situation is almost guaranteed to inhibit convergence or indeed any major innovation which imples a shift away from conventional costing and funding structures. Where innovations have occurred in higher education, it is usually the academic and support staff who carry the extra burden in terms of time needed to plan and carry through projects to completion.

Rumble (1986) outlines an alternative method of costing which may go some way towards alleviating these problems. His activity costing system was designed for Deakin University, Australia, which already operates a programme of which convergence of campus-based and distance education is a central feature. Rumble's model budgets in terms of clearly defined activities rather than in terms of staff and non-staff costs as is historically the case.

> The overall aim for a budgeting and accounting system geared to the production of activity-based costs must be to code expenditure to development, production and presentation costs by course and, at a higher level of aggregation, by program and supra-program. (p. 24)

The important feature of this alternative is that it is not restricted to distance education though it does incorporate some of its essential elements. In moves towards convergence, these elements would also become essential to mainstream departments and institutions.

**Academic Teaching Loads.** Traditional costing systems provide few incentives for academic staff to engage in lengthy periods of course preparation. In those higher education institutions which operate in the dual mode, workload is determined on the basis of mainstream costing, which focuses heavily on course presentation (i.e. teaching) with a minimal time allowance for course preparation.

Thus an academic who is credited with a workload of say one hundred Effective Full-Time Student Equivalents (EFTSs), twenty of whom are distance education students, will expect to allot the same time for course preparation and presentation to all students. The extra time needed for preparing materials and scheduling teaching activities for the distance education students represents a workload over and above that which is officially recognized by the institution.

This situation can only be altered at the administrative level and is closely related to costing and funding systems. If these remain unaltered then an obvious solution is to provide incentives for academic staff to engage in distance education or other forms of innovation. In some institutions, this is done by the provision of fellowships for course preparation whereby the distance education section uses funds to 'buy out' academic staff so that they may engage in a period of uninterrupted development work. Alternatively academic staff may be paid to prepare courses on an overload basis.

Such schemes have their pitfalls, as those who have administered them will be well aware: course preparation fellowships do not always attract academic staff who are genuinely interested in distance education - they may be seeking to take refuge from their home departments or looking for opportunities to enhance their publication records. Heads of departments may be reluctant to release productive and reliable staff because this would jeopardize their campus-based programme. Payment of academic staff on an overload basis is workable but in some cases it may result in a reduced commitment to other campus-based teaching and research activities.

The solution of spreading course preparation effort over a larger number of students, say to include part-time evening students, would give an incentive to teaching staff to engage in course preparation, provided that their face-to-face teaching loads were thereby reduced. Many academics are now realizing the value of this strategy but unless it receives official endorsement, at least at the departmental level, they are in the invidious position of being seen by their peers to be 'skimping on teaching'.

**Systems of Academic Promotion: Implications for Teaching.** Regardless of the intrinsic satisfaction which academics derive from teaching, they are still bound to institutions of higher education by extrinsic rewards, principally the method of promotion from one level to another.

Promotion criteria are are usually stated publicly by institutions, but to academics there sometimes appears to be a hiatus between such public statements and actual promotion criteria. In a study which examined the characteristics and values of Australian academics in universities and colleges of advanced education (CAEs) in 1978, Bowden and Anwyl (1983) were concerned with academic staff perceptions of what would be an **ideal** reward structure compared with their perceptions of the **actual** reward structure in their institutions. They noted that the job specification of university staff requires both teaching and research functions whereas that of college staff emphasizes teaching. In general respondents to the survey reflected these terms of appointment, with university staff being more likely to say that their interests were either mainly in research, or both teaching and research but leaning to research (49 per cent), compared with 13 per cent of college academics. On the other hand, college academics were more likely to say that their interests were mainly in teaching, or in both research and teaching but leaning to teaching (70 per cent), compared with 25 per cent of university staff.

Interestingly the survey also showed that:

> ... college staff are less fixed in their teaching methods than their university counterparts: CAE respondents reported that they use the lecture method less regularly; they are more likely to modify the traditional format when they do lecture; and they use a variety of small group teaching techniques. The attitudes of CAE staff on assessment matters are also less traditional than those of university teachers.
> (p. 44)

Moreover college staff were more likely to have participated in an inservice course designed to assist them to improve their teaching. This does not imply that university staff are indifferent to teaching. In fact both groups thought that in promotion they should be judged on the roles they actually performed, and for university staff this included teaching as well as research.

Interestingly enough though, only about one third of staff **in both sectors** believed that teaching effectiveness was an important criterion in determining salary and promotion. Most university staff believed that research was the only really important criterion and college staff believed that committee work and seniority were the important determinants. Similar results were reported by Halsey (1979) in a survey of British academics.

With regard to distance education and part-time studies, Bowden and Anwyl (1983) reported the following attitudes:

182

College academics were much stronger in their support of ready availability of external studies. More CAE respondents (45 per cent) opposed the view that it was an inferior form of study than supported it (33 per cent). The exact reverse was true of university respondents. University respondents did not take that negative view of part-time studies, but again college respondents were more strongly supportive. Part-time study is clearly a far more acceptable form of study than external studies. (pp. 53-4)

In a separate study, de Rome, Boud and Genn (1985) examined changes in academic staff perceptions of the relative importance of teaching and research in a large Australian university over the period 1973-82. They argued that morale and institutional health would be affected negatively if there were a gap between the stated promotion policies of institutions and the perceived practices of institutions. In particular where teaching excellence is a stated goal but appears not to feature prominently in the reward structure, low morale could be expected in those academics who emphasize teaching: their attitudes will be at variance with what they perceive to be those of the institution.

Over the nine-year period of this study, there had been a growing emphasis on academic staff development in universities, much of which was concerned with ways of assisting academics to teach well. Higher education units of various kinds have sprung up in most universities over that time and their roles have been primarily institutional research, staff induction, development of teaching skills, and staff evaluation.

In terms of academics' perceptions of an ideal situation, there was a decrease in the importance of teaching in the reward structure during the period studied. On the other hand the ideal importance of research as an activity increased over that period. Attitudes to committee and other administrative services did not change significantly.

In terms of perceptions of the actual importance of teaching in the reward structure, this decreased over time. The authors comment:

> Probably the most striking aspect ( ... ) is the very low
> percentage of staff perceiving high importance to be
> attached to anything to do with teaching, in contrast
> to the high to extremely high percentages associated
> with research related matters. (p. 136)

These findings do not relate to the promotion system *per se*
but to the academics' perceptions of it. It is these perceptions
that will influence the way in which academics behave and
consequently the health of an institution. As the authors point
out, this has occurred at a time when:

> ... conditions affecting the career prospects and
> mobility of academic staff appear to be deteriorating
> and the reward structure ( ... ) [is] increasingly
> important for maintaining and enhancing the
> professional viability of staff. (p. 139)

In part the problem may be attributable to the fact that
few academics really know how much value is placed on the
various criteria in any given promotion decision. Clearly it is
easier to evaluate research publications than to discern levels of
teaching excellence: campus-based teaching is essentially a
private activity. Cannon (1983) suggested that this may
explain the apparent failure of initiatives to improve teaching
in Australian universities.

Such initiatives have frequently been directed at individual
academics rather than senior adminstrators or departmental
heads. Since it is the context within which academics work
that shapes their behaviour as least as much as their individual
initiatives, Bowden and Anwyl (1983) predict, I believe rightly,
that staff development initiatives of this kind will not succeed.

The outcomes of these studies are pertinent to the issue of
how to enhance the quality of both distance education and
campus-based education and to the convergence of these
modes. If mainstream, campus-based teaching activities are
perceived by academics as being devalued compared to other

184

activities such as research, and if this perception influences their priorities, then we would expect distance teaching and innovation in teaching to be even lower down on their list of priorities. The increased demands which these activities make and the fact they they require a break with established teaching practices, mean that they are less likely to be adopted with enthusiasm within the reward system as it is currently perceived.

The rhetoric of institutions may encourage this effort but if it is not perceived as a source of reward then a certain amount of cynicism among academics is inevitable.

## Staff Perceptions of Mainstream and Distance Education

In a paper which examines academic staff perceptions of distance education versus campus-based teaching, Clark, Soliman and Sungaila (1984) focus on ways in which academic staff in a large dual-mode university perceive distance education, and on teaching areas where academics thought staff development was required.

The University of New England, Australia, where this study was conducted, has a major commitment to distance education: hence a high proportion of the academic staff are involved in it. The analysis is concerned mainly with the 82.3 per cent of the 124 respondents who were involved in both modes.

Not surprisingly, most respondents found distance teaching more demanding than campus-based teaching. The authors comment:

> This may be a reflection of a variety of factors such as experience, work load, and the time needed to develop such courses which is often not recognised in work load distributions. (p. 86)

In general though those who found distance teaching more demanding also found it more enjoyable.

Few academics disagreed with the statement that distance teaching had a beneficial effect on their campus-based teaching,

185

and benefits in the reverse direction were also perceived.

From these results it appears that, in general, academic staff at the University of New England have adjusted well to the task of teaching in a dual-mode institution. This institution has been engaged in distance education for several decades and currently more than half of its student population study in the distance education mode, so the viability of the University depends on these students to a large extent.

If one looks closely at the institutional context, however, some reasons for this degree of satisfaction emerge: distance education courses are well established and course preparation methods are quite basic, though compulsory residential schools do impose an extra burden on teaching staff.

This is quite a different situation from other established institutions of higher education, some of which have made serious attempts to redevelop their distance education courses and to engage in extensive use of telecommunications technology in teaching.

At the moment we have very little formal information about the impact of innovation in these institutions. Informal evidence derived from educational developers and distance education administrators suggests that there is a fairly high degree of staff resistance, particularly in institutions where course preparation and presentation were previously routinized to a large extent.

Smith (1980) makes this point with regard to established institutions.

> Some older established institutions which have been teaching externally for several decades have depended more on academic intuition than specialist staff or systematic procedures to develop external courses. **While it is much more difficult to introduce changes where the original blueprint has been successful in broad terms,** such institutions must adjust to changing circumstances and different expectations if their products are to be compared favourably with others. (pp. 66-7, my emphasis)

## Student Perceptions of Convergence

For students who are remote from an institution, convergence of distance education and mainstream education implies that attempts will be made to offset some of the disadvantages of distance education as it is currently practised by introducing some of the positive features of campus-based instruction. Telecommunications technology makes this an achievable goal. Distance education could move along the teacher-unsupported/teacher-supported continuum to a significant degree, providing more support for distance education students than is currently the case.

For campus-based students the shift along the continuum would be in the reverse direction: towards more independence from their teachers and towards assuming greater responsibility for their own learning.

There is no reason to suppose that either of these groups of students would welcome such changes even though they should provide them with opportunities for an enhanced learning experience. In fact it is reasonable to assume that the students themselves will create barriers to convergence by rejecting those innovations which their teachers have so carefully planned and possibly fought a good many hard-won institutional battles to bring about.

**Distance Education Students.** In so far as distance education students tend to be adults in middle life, it is assumed that they will adapt well to the distance education mode: they do not need the same degree of teacher support which is available to campus-based students and can be expected to study in a relatively unsupported manner.

Moreover several research studies have concluded that adults approach learning in a relatively independent way, use wholistic strategies (Säljö, 1982) and that they analyse learning materials at a deeper level than younger students, searching for meaning and relating what they learn to their own experience (Watkins and Hattie, 1985; Watkins, 1986). They also seem to be intrinsically motivated, particularly those who are studying in the humanities.

187

Whereas once it might have been assumed that students undertook distance education courses only because no other alternatives were available to them, it is now assumed that many students choose this mode of study because of the freedom from constraints which it affords. A high proportion of distance education students are not geographically isolated but reside in cities where opportunities for campus-based, part-time or full-time study exist.

There is, however, evidence that some of these assumptions are open to question. A 1983 survey of students studying at a distance from the University of Queensland (Kelly, 1986) casts some doubt on the assumption that most adult distance education students actually prefer this mode of study and that most are studying for intrinsic satisfaction.

A high proportion of respondents to this survey (55 per cent) said they were studying for utilitarian reasons: to improve employment and career opportunities. This was particularly true of students enrolled in Education and Commerce/Economics courses. It was also more true for students below forty-five years of age than for older students.

When asked about previous study experiences only 30 per cent of the respondents had never studied on campus, and these tended to be concentrated in the older group above forty-five years of age, so many had an image of what campus-based education was like.

Most interesting of all was the fact that only **17 per cent** of respondents said they would prefer not to study on campus at all. The remaining students expressed a preference for full-time on-campus study (39 per cent), part-time on-campus study (19 per cent), or for some campus-based study combined with distance education study (25 per cent). A preference for studying only in the distance education mode was unrelated to student characteristics such as age, sex, degree enrolled, grade point average or place of residence. Thus though 23 per cent of the respondents actually lived in the Brisbane metropolitan area where the University of Queensland is located, they were as inclined as students in all other regions to say that they would prefer some kind of campus-based education.

What the majority of the students seemed to be saying was that they would prefer to study in a mainstream, campus environment with the degree of teacher support and peer group support that this is assumed to provide. In part, the responses reflect a desire to progress more quickly through the course by full-time study, but a proportion of students opted for part-time on-campus or a mixed-mode alternative.

In this survey I also looked at the way in which students responded to the extensive network of regional support services which the University of Queensland provides, and to the increased use of technology in teaching. In general the survey revealed that regional support services were highly valued by those who used them but that these services were under-utilized even by students who had ready access to them.

On the other hand, a high proportion of students had contact with their teachers (67 per cent) either by mail, telephone or face-to-face visits.

When it came to using technology for teaching, respondents were either lukewarm or uninformed about the possibilities. Only 3.3 per cent had taken part in telephone tutorials during the year. Asked whether they would like to take part in telephone tutorials in the future, 67 per cent of students said that the idea did not appeal to them or that they did not know enough about telephone tutorials to comment.

Access to technology which might be used in teaching was also quite low at the time of the survey. Only 23 per cent of respondents owned or leased a video-recorder though an additional number had plans to purchase one or said they would be able to arrange access if required.

Personal computers were owned or leased by 13 per cent of respondents though some were either planning to purchase one or could arrange access if required.

What emerged from this survey was a high degree of campus orientation combined with a relatively low degree of regional orientation (particularly amongst men) and an even lower degree of technological orientation (particularly amongst women).

The process of convergence in distance education by using technology to enhance teacher support will not be a straightforward matter in these circumstances, particularly where a high proportion of students may really want some mainstream campus-based education of a traditional kind.

**Campus-based Students.** What happens when campus-based students, mainly young undergraduates, are confronted with a teaching innovation which aims to make them less dependent on their teachers? The recent transition in the Department of Chemical Engineering at the University of Queensland, Australia, from face-to-face teaching to resource-based education throws some light on this question.

In a progress report on the innovation, Leung (1985) describes resource-based education (RBE) as follows:

> RBE involves the provision of a range of resources to assist students in their self-learning. The resources include open laboratories, hardware display laboratories, computer-aided learning materials, written notes, video material and books. The resources will be made available to students during long opening hours under supervision by academic staff. The number of lectures for each subject will be reduced with emphasis on fundamentals. Students are expected to progress in a self-paced manner with some regulations to ensure that set goals are achieved within a specific time. (Pages unnumbered)

This initiative arose from the Department's review of its curriculum and teaching methods in 1983. A five year plan was developed with resource-based education being introduced progressively by subjects from 1985 onwards. Financial support for the project was provided by a number of companies. Outcomes were monitored by the University's Tertiary Education Institute.

It should be noted that the introduction of resource-based education was paralleled by other changes which were not, strictly speaking, related to the method: a revised curriculum, continuous and group-based assessment, use of computer-aided learning.

190

In a paper which reports the results of monitoring the project, Isaacs (1986) takes particular note of the ways in which students perceived the new resource-based subjects. Students were questioned on a number of issues related to the method, including their preference for it as opposed to mainstream methods with which they were familiar, and on the value of resource-based education in general.

At the stage of Isaacs's survey, three resource-based subjects had been introduced sequentially, with many of the respondents having taken more than one of these subjects in addition to other subjects which were still being taught by face-to-face lectures.

For the first subject introduced, two out of twenty-seven students were in favour of the method, one thought that a combination of methods was needed and twenty-four students favoured what they referred to as a 'conventional approach'.

What was wrong with the resource-based approach? A common theme seemed to be that students could no longer ascertain what the lecturer wanted them to know in the subject. This is despite the detailed sets of behavioural objectives which were prepared for each module in the subject. Apparently what was missing from the students' point of view was the emphasis on particular aspects of the work which frequently comes across in the lecture situation.

Other complaints were that students in the class were all progressing at different rates, that the workload was too heavy, that it was difficult to motivate oneself, or that the particular subject was too difficult to teach using a resource-based approach.

Isaacs quotes one student who appeared to sum up the difficulties that most were experiencing.

It is simply a lot easier to be spoon fed material in the conventional manner. Resource based courses are fine and probably more effective, but they take too much time. In a very hard semester, like this, resource based subjects tend to get neglected in favour of other more pressing requirements. (pp. 3-4)

Some students thought that in introducing resource-based education the academic staff were just 'copping out' of their real teaching responsibilities!

When the second subject was introduced there was a more favourable response though eighteen of the thirty students interviewed still favoured a conventional approach. (More face-to-face lectures were given in this subject than in the previous one.)

In the third subject, seventeen of the thirty-six students still favoured a conventional approach.

The image of what resource-based education is became blurred because students had to deal with the introduction of continuous and group-based assessment and computer-aided learning at the same time. Some thought that these features were an integral part of resource-based education and, because they were negatively disposed towards one of them, they responded negatively to the whole idea. Several students disliked group-based assessment intensely for example, and saw this as a necessary feature of resource-based education, which it is not.

Setting behavioural objectives had the desired effect of making students work hard to achieve them, but on the negative side they tended to underrate their achievement and considered the workload to be excessive. This highlights the amount of cue-seeking behaviour that students engage in and which has been documented in other research (Miller and Parlett, 1974).

The staff who developed the programme now realize that they needed to 'sell' the idea to students much more than they had done at first, and Isaacs comments that both staff and students appeared to be adjusting their behaviours to accommodate each other.

The evaluation of the programme highlights some of the assumptions on which students rely in campus-based education of a traditional kind. The guidance given in face-to-face lectures is apparently important in shaping learning behaviours and in knowing how to select those elements of the subject which are really important. Written objectives do not necessarily fulfil this role.

One would expect that older students might adjust more readily to this kind of innovation in that they would be willing to pursue their own objectives, but it is a mistake to assume that cue-seeking behaviour is absent in adults. Many who return to study after a period of years may bring with them the attitudes to learning and assessment which were formed in their youth.

Some would argue that the responses of the students in this project were typical of science and technology students but not of those in the arts and social sciences, where teaching has always been resource-based in the sense that students need to rely heavily on resources outside lectures to complete the course and the number of face-to-face lectures provided is small compared with science courses. It seems to me that this misses the point of resource-based education. It is not the number of contact hours *per se* that is important, nor the amount of time students spend in independent study in the library, but it is the degree of guidance and teacher support that students receive in lectures that seems to be the important component of campus-based education.

Whether the absence of this kind of guidance was one of the reasons why the distance education students surveyed by Kelly (1986) preferred campus-based education is not known, but it is a question which deserves further research effort.

## Political Barriers to Convergence

Distance education in Australia has received a fair amount of attention from federal government committees. In particular three reports deal with planning in the context of tertiary and higher education: Karmel (1973); Johnson (1983); Commonwealth Tertiary Education Commission (1986).

In none of these reports is there any indication that their authors have contemplated a system of education which does not preserve rigid boundaries between distance education and campus-based education.

The Karmel report deals with the unmet demand for tertiary education in Australia and suggests ways in which this demand might be met. Two options are considered: the establishment of a national institution which would teach only at a distance; and enhancement of the existing dual-mode system.

The first option was rejected on the grounds that such an institution '... might actually reduce the likelihood of existing institutions adopting innovatory policies; they might reasonably take the view that open education was being looked after by a specific body' (p. 80).

Instead the recommendation was for the alternative of '... infusing the tertiary educational system as a whole with a greater measure of openness than currently exists' (p. 80).

The Karmel report also recommended the establishment of a National Institute of Open Tertiary Education, a national statutory body that would work to: facilitate access to tertiary institutions; to maintain and expand opportunities for part-time and 'off-campus' study; to survey community needs; to oversee provision of distance education courses nationally; to facilitate services for distance education students. This proposal was allowed to lapse in the economic downturn in the years after the report was released.

The value of this report is that it treats distance education seriously as a credible alternative to campus-based education and that it sees the potential of distance education as a means of facilitating access to tertiary education. Unlike subsequent reports, it was not obsessively concerned with issues of the cost of distance education.

While the Karmel report indicates that it is desirable to expand the range of teaching methods used in distance education, using technology in the widest sense, there is no indication that compartmentalism of tertiary education into full-time, part-time and off-campus was seen as either undesirable or unnecessary. The methods of mainstream education are left intact apart from recommendations concerning access and transfer of credit among institutions.

Ten years later, Johnson (1983) specifically investigated the provision of 'external studies' in higher education in a report prepared for the Commonwealth Tertiary Education Commission.

Over the period that spans the appearance of the two reports, there was an expansion in the number of institutions which offered distance education courses and the number of students who were undertaking them.

Johnson notes the different demands on academics of distance education and campus-based education.

> I doubt if a teacher in the internal mode would need to put so much effort beforehand into preparing a course unless it were a completely new course with all new material; preparation of the individual lectures proceeds while the course is being offered. (p. 18)

He also notes that while the dual-mode system has certain educational advantages, it makes it difficult to achieve economies of scale similar to those which the British Open University has been able to achieve by enrolling very large numbers of students in relatively few courses.

In terms of provision of distance education courses, Johnson claims, rightly, that there are marked areas of under-provision. At the same time the number of institutions involved and the number of courses offered has resulted in many similar courses being offered around the nation. This he views as unnecessary duplication.

> There is no national overview, no coordination of the activities of the states, no matter how close the coordination within each state. Yet of all aspects of education, external (or, as it is often called, 'distance') education is the one which is most obviously suited to a nationwide policy on provision. One wonders for instance whether the nation needs quite so many courses in teacher education, even allowing for all the specialisms and all the institutional loyalties. One wonders about the economies of scale and the quality of materials that might result with more concentration of effort. (p. 25)

Furthermore,

> Given the lack of a well-considered policy and a nationally coordinated plan, or even a body whose responsibility it is to devise such a policy and plan, the CTEC can only express its concern and request institutions not already active in the field not to enter it. (pp. 25-6)

Most telling of all is Johnson's suspicion about the motives of specific institutions which plan to offer campus-based courses in a non-traditional way. He cites the cases of a number of institutions,

> ... all of which involve the expansion of their activities in provision for students who are not standard on-campus students. (p. 26)

That these courses might represent important innovations in Australian higher education (as is the case with Griffith University, which Johnson specifically names), aimed at blurring the boundaries between the two modes, is not an alternative which he considers. Convergence is seen merely as an attempt to get into external studies 'by the back door'.

Finally the *Review of Efficiency and Effectiveness in Higher Education* (1986), prepared by the Commonwealth Tertiary Education Commission, devotes a chapter to 'External Studies'. This contains a number of detailed recommendations which, if implemented, could change the pattern of provision of distance education and will certainly serve to maintain a rigid distinction between distance education and campus-based education at a time when the boundaries are showing signs of dissolving.

The Commission acknowledges the advantages of the current arrangements for distance education in which providers are scattered throughout the country and in which academics teach both campus-based and distance education students. The Commission seems prepared to waive these advantages, however, because on the negative side the arrangement has resulted in '... a fragmentation of resources and unnecessary duplication of effort' (p. 222). A halfway measure between setting up a national provider which would enrol all 45,000 students currently enrolled in higher education courses at a distance in Australia, and the present dual-mode arrangement, is proposed.

Some institutions are to be designated as principal providers, others as specialist providers and others as limited providers who would eventually withdraw from the field altogether. In general, regional institutions are to become principal providers in order to guarantee their continued viability in the face of a decline in full-time enrolments, and metropolitan institutions are to become specialist providers or limited providers in order to accommodate more of the full-time students seeking places in them. Specialist providers will be required to relinquish their distance education infrastructures and use those of the principal providers.

Alternative solutions to the problems facing higher education and the particular problem of the high fixed costs associated with the preparation of distance education courses might have been examined in the report, but they were not. For instance, a viable alternative to partial dismantling of the dual-mode model would be to re-examine its potential afresh, putting aside a model which is loosely based on the example provided by the British Open University. The CTEC *Review* acknowledges that one positive aspect of the dual-mode model is that it provides opportunities for interaction between on- and off-campus teaching. If one wished to develop this situation further, the approach would be to encourage diversity and duplication in distance education courses so that they are spread over as wide a range of institutions as possible and to maintain a resident pool of distance education expertise in all these institutions rather than restricting it to a few. Secondly, moves could be made to encourage integration further, by, for example, using similar methods of teaching for all part-time students and moving in the direction of using some distance education methods in campus-based teaching.

It is unfortunate that the *Review* draws back from exploring alternatives such as these. Instead the authors have, perhaps unwittingly, chosen to maintain the rigid barriers between modes that have existed in the past.

In conclusion, this Chapter has dealt with a diverse range of issues surrounding the theme of convergence in Australian higher education. They all impact on any innovation of substance and some will have an impact on minor innovations.

It would be unwise to imagine that the perceptions of organizations, of academic staff and students or of government agencies will change suddenly in order to remove barriers to convergence.

Such attitudinal changes usually come about through a mixture of pragmatism and idealism and, in the present economic climate, significant innovations will obviously need financial backing from outside the federal government sector.

It is the public demand for initial education and further education combined with awareness that education is vital to maintaining and improving Australia's position in the world that will create the pragmatic reasons for justification of such new developments.

# References

Bowden, J.A. and Anwyl, J. (1983) 'Some Characteristics and Attitudes of Academics in Australian Universities and Colleges of Advanced Education', *Higher Education Research and Development*, **2**, 1, 39-61

Cannon, R.A. (1983) 'The Professional Development of Australian University Teachers: An Act of Faith?,' *Higher Education*, **12**, 1, 19-34

Clark, R.G., Soliman, M.H. and Sungaila, H.M. (1984) 'Staff Perceptions of External Versus Internal Teaching and Staff Development', *Distance Education*, **5**, 1, 84-92

Commonwealth Tertiary Education Commission (1986) *Review of Efficiency and Effectiveness in Higher Education*, Australian Government Publishing Service, Canberra

Griew, S. (1980) 'A Model for the Allocation and Utilisation of Academic Staff Resources', *Canadian Journal of Higher Education*, **10**, 2, 73-84

Guiton, P. (1982) 'Resource Allocation in the Australian Two-Mode University' in John S. Daniel, Martha A. Stroud and John R. Thompson (eds.), *Learning at a Distance: A World Perspective*, Athabasca University/ICCE, Edmonton, pp. 176-8

Halsey, A.H. (1979) 'A Tale of Two Systems: Field Studies', *The Times Higher Education Supplement*, 16.11.79, 20-1

Isaacs, G. (1986) 'Learner-oriented Subjects in a Teacher-oriented Course', Tertiary Education Institute, University of Queensland, Australia. To appear in Miller, A. H. and Sachse-Åkerlind, Gerlese (1987) 'The Learner in Higher Education: a Forgotten Species?', *Research and Development in Higher Education*, **9**, HERDSA, Sydney, 87-91 (In press)

Johnson, R. (1983) *The Provision of External Studies in Australian Higher Education*, report prepared for the Commonwealth Tertiary Education Commission, Canberra

Karmel, P. (1973) *Open Tertiary Education in Australia*, report of the Committee on Open University to the Australian Universities Commission, Canberra

Keegan, D. (1980) 'On Defining Distance Education', *Distance Education*, **1**, 1, 13-36

Kelly, M.E. (1986) 'A Survey of Use and Evaluation of Support Sevices by External Students', *Working Papers in Distance Education*, No. 10, School of External Studies and Continuing Education, University of Queensland, Brisbane

Leung, L.S. (1985) *Resource Based Education in Chemical Engineering, Progress Report 1984-1985*, Department of Chemical Engineering, University of Queensland, Brisbane

Miller, C.M.L. and Parlett, M. (1974) *Up to the Mark: a Study of the Examination Game*, Society for Research into Higher Education, London

Rome, E. de, Boud, D. and Genn, J.M. (1985) 'Changes in Academic Staff Perceptions of the Status of Teaching and Research', *Higher Education Research and Development*, **4**, 2, 131-43

Rumble, G. (1986) 'Activity Costing in Mixed-mode Institutions: a Report Based on a Study of Deakin

University', *Deakin Open Education Monograph No. 2*, Geelong

Rumble, G. and Harry, K. (1982) *The Distance Teaching Universities*, Croom Helm, London

Säljö, R. (1982) *Learning and Understanding*, Göteborg Studies in Educational Sciences 41, Acta Universitatis Gothoburgensis

Shaw, B. and Taylor, J. (1984) 'Instructional Design: Distance Education and Academic Tradition', *Distance Education*, **3**, 2, 277-85

Smith, K.C. (1980) 'Course Development Procedures', *Distance Education*, **1**, 1, 61-7

Watkins, D. (1986) 'The Approaches to Learning of Australian Tertiary Students: A Replication', *Higher Education Research and Development*, **5**, 2, 185-90

Watkins, D. and Hattie, J. (1985) 'A Longitudinal Study of the Learning Processes of Tertiary Students', *Human Learning*, **4**, 127-41

**Mavis E. Kelly**, MA *Syd.*, PhD *Monash*

Course Development Adviser
School of External Studies and Continuing Education
University of Queensland
Australia

# AUTHOR INDEX

# SUBJECT INDEX